DESMOND FENNELL

HIS LIFE AND WORK

DESMOND FENNELL

HIS LIFE AND WORK

edited by Toner Quinn

VERITAS

Published 2001 by
Veritas Publications
7/8 Lower Abbey Street
Dublin 1
Ireland

Email publications@veritas.ie
Website www.veritas.ie

ISBN 1 85390 509 7

A catalogue record for this book is available from the British Library.

Veritas books are printed on paper made from the wood pulp of managed forests. For every tree felled, at least one tree is planted, thereby renewing natural resources.

Cover photographs © Irish Independent
Cover design by Pierce Design
Printed in the Republic of Ireland by Betaprint Ltd, Dublin

CONTENTS

CONTRIBUTORS

Brian Arkins was educated at Clongowes Wood College and UCD, where he obtained an MA in Classics and a PhD in Latin. He is the author of six books of criticism including *Sexuality in Catullus* and *Builders of My Soul: Greek and Roman Themes in Yeats*.

John Waters is a journalist and editor and for the past ten years has been a columnist with the *Irish Times*. He is the author of four books – *Jiving at the Crossroads, Every Day Like Sunday?, Race of Angels: Ireland and the Genesis of U2* and *An Intelligent Person's Guide to Modern Ireland*. He has also written several plays for stage and radio, including *Long Black Coat, Easter Dues* and *Holy Secrets*. He has a daughter, Roisín, and lives in Dublin.

Nollaig Ó Gadhra lectured in communications and Irish and European studies in Galway RTC for twenty-five years. His paper on 'The Future of the Irish Gaeltacht Communties in the 21st Century', which he delivered at the nineteenth Harvard *University Celtic Colloqium*, will soon be published in Ireland.

Prof. J.J. Lee is Head of the Department of History at University College Cork, where he has also served terms as Dean of Arts and Vice-President since his appointment as Professor of Modern History in 1974. Prof. Lee's publications on Irish, European and American History include *Ireland 1912–1985* (Cambridge, 1990), which was awarded the Aer Lingus/Irish Times Prize for Literature, as well as the Donnelly Prize of the American Conference for Irish Studies, and the Sunday Independent/Irish Life Prize for History.

Risteárd Ó Glaisne was born in Bandon, County Cork, in 1927 and became a secondary school teacher, freelance journalist and broadcaster. He is the author of twenty-six books, almost all in Irish. His latest publication is entitled *Dí-armáil nó Díothú: Éire, an Eoraip, an Domhain*, published by Coiscéim.

Mary Cullen is a former Senior Lecturer in Modern History at NUI Maynooth. At present she is a Research Associate at the Centre for Gender and Women's Studies at Trinity College, Dublin, where she teaches in the M. Phil. programme. She has published extensively in women's history.

Bob Quinn is a film-maker, writer and photographer. His films include Poitín, the Atlantean trilogy, Budawanny, and Navigatio. His most recent book is entitled *Maverick: A Dissident View of Broadcasting Today*, published by Brandon.

Carrie Crowley presents the interview series, *Snapshots*, every Sunday morning on RTÉ Radio 1. The programme is produced by Liz Sweeney.

EDITOR'S PREFACE

GIVEN THE range of subject matter which Desmond Fennell has tackled in a lifetime of writing, this book could have originated from almost any publisher in Ireland. As it happens, the venture has been undertaken by a 'religious publisher'. This is only partly because religion is one of the subjects Fennell has frequently touched on. This editor believes that a crucial role of religious publishing is to stimulate (wide-ranging) consideration of the contemporary moral and intellectual climate. In recent years this has been a developing part of Veritas' work.

The single most attractive aspect of producing a commentary on Desmond Fennell and his work has been this: such is the depth of the writer's probings that in commenting on or discussing any aspect of his work – no matter how minor – a conscientious essayist must take on many of the 'larger questions'.

Fennell's work is the ideal fulcrum for good debate. It is unambiguous, erudite and profound, always challenging the conventional wisdom and suggesting alternative perceptions. It possesses, in a word, substance. And yet you will search Irish books and journals in vain for references to his work or any serious critique of his thought. Some of the essays refer to this phenomenon of omission.

Partly because of the lack of discussion about the writer, this editor was reluctant to pedantically carve Fennell's work up into sections or to ask the contributors to focus on a particular period or theme. Instead, it was hoped that their independent minds would supply free-ranging and original perspectives. In that, I think we have been successful.

Further, when this project was originally contemplated, it was feared that it might result in 'A Festschrift to Desmond Fennell'. Such a venture always implies an uncritical pat on the back and that was certainly never the plan. If anything, given that most of his books are now out of print, this publication was purely envisioned as an introduction, a starting point for those interested in the real world or simply curious about his work. It is certainly not meant to be the final word – and I do not think it will be.

Toner Quinn
Editor
Veritas Publications
October 2001

INTRODUCTION

DESMOND FENNELL:
AN UNORTHODOX VOICE

BRIAN ARKINS

EVERY SOCIETY needs a particular ideology, both in its day-to-day practices and its long-term goals. The term applied to those who embrace ideology is often 'orthodox', which means 'of opinion or doctrine: right, correct, true'. But this begs the question, who decides what is 'orthodox' at a given moment, and suggests that we may need critics of the prevailing ideology of the day. Desmond Fennell is our most noted example of that sort of writer, who consistently challenges the orthodox views held in Ireland and the world generally. This essay seeks to delineate briefly his achievement in presenting that challenge to opinions that are generally held.

After the formation of the Irish Free State in 1922, it became imperative to implement a number of key aims. The first aim, and one that was later to be least controversial, was to take over the administration of the State from the British. This was not so simple as might have appeared because of a Civil War between forces pro and anti the Treaty with Britain, and it is a tribute to both sides that smooth transitions of power took place.

The next goal for the Irish Free State was economic, and here there was much less success. Indeed, for the greater part of the twentieth century, high unemployment and high emigration were the order of the day. It is not until the Celtic Tiger economy of the 1990s that the economic problem was solved.

Two other goals were prominent in the Irish Free State: the reunification of Ireland, and the restoration of the Irish language. Neither of these goals was achieved. Both are examined critically by Fennell in penetrating essays.

As time went by, from the 1960s on, a new ideology entered Irish society, to which the term 'liberal' is often applied. This does not so much refer to economic doctrines – as in the liberalism of Adam Smith – as to an individualistic and consumer approach to life that stresses the vital importance of the individual person, and especially the economic and sexual freedom of that person. This 'liberal agenda' has been advanced in Ireland by the entity known as 'Dublin 4', a powerful lobby group based in Dublin. A main part of Fennell's critique of contemporary orthodoxy in Ireland is directed at this new liberalism.

The goals of the Irish Free State – political, economic, linguistic – were large ones, and however unrealistic, were in themselves worthwhile, stressing society rather than the individual person. What Fennell misses in our present set up is coherent goals of that nature, as 'the reassembled Irish mind creating ideas, lives and literature, and generating courageous action.' Indeed he feels that his present unorthodox ideas 'rank as thought-crime', as in Orwell's *Nineteen Eighty-Four*.[1]

Unlike most Irish people, Desmond Fennell went to live for a number of years in the Gaeltacht (at Maoinis, near Carna in Conamara). He is therefore fully familiar with the problems associated with Irish, in which he is fluent. Fennell is fully realistic about the Gaeltacht (unlike some other people): he found the Irish-speaking population had shrunk to 29,000 in 1975, and notes that 'the end of the Gaeltacht is now in sight.'[2]

But Fennell is also keenly aware of the loss of Irish in the Gaeltacht areas and indeed throughout Ireland. When Fennell points out that a community imposes meaning on a landscape through names (as in Friel's play *Translations*), he suggests the Sapir-Whorf hypothesis that a particular language constructs reality in its own way. For that reason, one language is not as good as another, and the loss of Irish is a shocking cultural event (is there a precedent for it?).

Hence Fennell says of the thought '*Níl aon mhaith leis an nGaeilge*' (Irish is no good) that 'it was the poisoned pen inserted into the eagle's body four centuries ago, in places like north County Dublin, south Wexford and east Down, and never removed.'[3]

Writing in 1991, Fennell held that the Northern Ireland violence 'will be ended, ultimately, as it could have been years ago, by decisive political measures giving due recognition to both communities.'[4] This goal, which is that enshrined in the Good Friday Agreement of 1998, shows that Fennell's thought about Northern Ireland is very far from being simplistically pro-nationalist.

Fennell starts from the premiss that there are two historic peoples in Northern Ireland, 'people of the Gaelic and Irish Catholic tradition', and 'people of the Scotto-British and protestant tradition',[6] and that the conflict is what relative states and power each people should have. Fennell proposed 'a political reconstruction of the North based on a western and an eastern region, which would contain, respectively, a Catholic and a Protestant majority' (like Swiss cantons).[5] Basic to this position and transcending it is that each people must be allowed to coexist peacefully and be guaranteed an adequate share of political power.

Fennell fully recognises the validity of the position of the unionists, whom he terms Ulster British, as well as of the

nationalists, whom he terms Six-County Irish. These terms
stress that the conflict in Northern Ireland is not a religious, but
an ethnic one, in which the Six-County Irish were struggling for
the right 'to be Irish in their part of Ireland'.[6] Equally well,
Fennell saw that the proposals from Sinn Féin for a four-
province federation must involve recognition of the Ulster
British identity. It is worth stressing that the Dublin
establishment was often hostile to this concept of ethnic
plurality, especially in regard to the unionists. Worth stressing
too how much of Fennell's basic thinking on the North
(evolved over many years) is in accord with that lying behind
the Good Friday Agreement.

Fennell's analysis of how consumer capitalism penetrated
Ireland from the 1960s on is one of the best things he has done.[7]
In a revulsion against all that has previously been valued,
Ireland embraced 'a mishmash of undigested elements' from
America and Britain, and, in particular, the economic and
sexual 'rights' of the individual person. Everything is now
reduced to what is economic and what can be consumed: the
central issue was that 'atomisation, massification and
materialisation proceeded, and that production, consumption,
and money flow increased.'[8] The battle was most obviously
fought in the sexual area: sex was a commodity like everything
else, and had to be readily available.

The results of this materialism for Irish Catholicism, long
the hallmark of the country, were considerable. Since many
people became agnostic about non-material reality, the
Catholic Church's writ no longer ran so large, indeed consumer
capitalism, in the shape in particular of television and the *Irish
Times,* was strongly opposed to theistic attitudes.

This agenda of consumer capitalism has been advanced in
Ireland by the mentality known as Dublin 4, which Fennell
describes as 'a powerful social group with a characteristic

mentality and agenda . . . exists largely outside parliament and the government of the day, but includes varying proportions of both.'⁹ To be equated with the 'chattering classes' in London and with the State class in Black African countries, Dublin 4 backs Ireland's membership of the European Union; seeks to free Ireland from the grip of nationalist history and of Catholicism; is specially hostile to the populism of Fianna Fáil; and, in general, feels itself different from the rest of the country. Though it must be said that the majority of the media – newspapers, radio, television – is now on the side of Dublin 4.

Fennell waxes eloquent about the 'liberal agenda':

> This boiled down to divorce, more condoms, easy on abortion; support the EC, unionist demands, British policy in the North and revisionist history-writing; bash Charles Haughey, Fianna Fáil, the Catholic Church, the Constitution, the IRA, Sinn Féin, the GAA, Irish Americans, and all those ignorant, deluded people in northside Dublin and 'rural Ireland' (the rest of the Republic) who support that sinister man or one of those benighted organisations.¹⁰

Clearly, then, Fennell sees Dublin 4 as a regressive entity that opposes the 150-year-old endeavour 'to achieve and maintain the intellectual, cultural and political autonomy of the Irish nation in all of Ireland.'¹¹ That this group likes to think of itself as 'progressive' derives of course from the fact that Dublin 4 people see themselves as rational and good as opposed to the unenlightened and bad. A comparison with the supporters of the French Revolution is not inapposite, indeed Dublin 4 is a sort of inverted Church with its own ayatollahs.

One of Fennell's most controversial essays is that on Seamus Heaney, whom Edward Lucie-Smith sees as 'the yardstick against which other poets, of the same generation or younger, must measure their own success.'[12] Even though Fennell may seem unduly prescriptive for poets, his essay raises very serious questions about Irish poetry and about Heaney's reputation.

To begin with, there is the category of 'Northern poet'. It is widely assumed that such a category exists, but, if this is so, then logically a category called 'Southern poet' should also exist. Apparently, however, this is not the case, with the result that the designation 'Northern poet' is somewhat specious. Indeed the existence of the entity 'Northern poet' has led to a downplaying of a considerable number of poets from the Republic of Ireland, such as Desmond Egan, James Liddy, Desmond O'Grady, and Paula Meehan.

A further aspect of 'Northern' poets, and, in particular, Heaney, is their mode of reception. Heaney's career is indeed exemplary: he is a lyric poet published by Faber and Faber in London, taken up on the East coast of America, and championed by an important American critic (Helen Vendler). Fennell then links Heaney's type of poetry with the New Puritanism and with consumer capitalism that 'aspires to no transcendence'.[13] We are dealing with the music of what happens.

The central issue with Heaney is not whether he is a good poet, for this seems undeniable, but whether he can sustain the extraordinary claims that are made for him. Helen Vendler, for example, has no hesitation in saying that he is 'as much the legitimate heir of Keats and Frost as of Kavanagh or Yeats.'[14]

Fennell identifies two central problems with Heaney. One is his notorious reluctance to use language as public speech, as comment on political matters in the North, with the result that his poetry lacks a communal dimension. What could be done in this vein is best seen in what is arguably Heaney's best volume *North* (1975), but he did not continue to address politics in this way. Noteworthy too is Heaney's reluctance to address aspects of life in the Republic of Ireland, where he has now lived for many years.

But a greater problem with Heaney is that shared by much modern verse. Often in his work, objects are presented as though they are important, but it is not all clear in what this importance lies. This may be called the debased epiphany, and seems common in Heaney's work. As Fennell says, in writing about Heaney's poems about married life or rural life, 'none of them contains any statement, plain or figurative, about those or related matters'. This version of 'The poem itself' links Heaney to the Movement and the Group in England. And is as reductive.[15]

In recent years, much of Fennell's energies have been devoted to what he calls postwestern civilisation. Central here is the bombing of the Japanese city of Hiroshima by America in 1945, which had killed 282,000 people by 1952. For Fennell, this is not just one atrocity among many (such as the Holocaust); rather, this use of the atomic bomb on unarmed, innocent civilians constitutes a supremely barbarous act, which brought to an end one era of civilisation, and brought into being another. What has happened is that the President of the West's leading power has ordered 'a great and sensational massacre'.[16]

Fennell here follows and goes beyond the famous editorial in the *Saturday Review* of 18 August, 1945, by Norman Cousins, in which he maintained that 'Modern Man is obsolete' and that 'a new age is born.' Or, as Desmond Egan puts it in his poem 'Hiroshima', 'Hiroshima your shadow burns/into the granite of history'.[17]

After Hiroshima, the rulers of the West withdrew support definitively from many key rules of social behaviour that characterised western civilisation, not least in regard to sexual behaviour. Part of what is going on here is withdrawal of the West from implicit commitment to the Christian religion and for recognising God as the supreme moral authority. Indeed the rulers of this American revolution (like their predecessors in France, Germany, and Russia) had 'a conviction of righteousness so absolute that they brooked no limitations, institutional, moral or physical, which appeared to them restrictive.'[18]

A large part of this new American revolution is the manufacture and possession of nuclear weapons, which is extremely expensive. To facilitate this programme, America depends on a constant flow of money in late consumer capitalism, which has made the country an economic superpower. But with all this comes, argues Fennell, 'moral chaos': 'An untried collection of rules and values thrown together in the interests of Superpower and a utopian dream must inevitably result in moral chaos, and therefore in a life that appears intrinsically "senseless".'

Such is Fennell's radical analysis of the wholly new era that we now live in, and of the moral vacuum that characterises it. This analysis is his most striking departure from current orthodoxy that condones and endorses our postwestern condition; it is Fennell at his most creative.

Notes

1. Desmond Fennell, *Heresy: The Battle of Ideas in Modern Ireland* (Belfast, 1993), xi-xii.
2. ibid., 3.
3. ibid., 8.
4. ibid., 143.
5. ibid., 98-99.
6. ibid., 103.
7. Desmond Fennell, *The State of the Nation* (Dublin, 1983), 80-103.

8.   ibid., 37;85.
9.   *Heresy: The Battle of Ideas in Modern Ireland*, 187.
10. ibid., 197.
11. ibid., 197-198.
12. ibid., 130-131.
13. ibid., 169.
14. ibid., 131.
15. ibid., 135.
16. Desmond Fennell, *The Postwestern Condition: Between Chaos and Civilisation* (London, 1999), 24.
17. Desmond Egan, *A Song for My Father* (Calstock/Newbridge, 1989), 22.
18. *The Postwestern Condition: Between Chaos and Civilisation*, 30.
19   ibid., 38.

DESMOND FENNELL AND THE POLITICS OF ERROR

JOHN WATERS

IN THE EARLY months of the new millennium, while talking one day on the phone with Desmond Fennell, I gathered that he was a little disgruntled about something. He explained that he had written an article for a national newspaper – the content of which I do not recall – and the editors had made a number of changes to the text without consulting him. He was particularly annoyed because he had been scrupulously careful to stay within the designated word count, so as to avoid providing any excuse for interference with the article. He found the incident most uncivil, he said, as well as frustrating and not a little embarrassing. The piece, as printed, did not convey what he intended, having had its meaning altered by the changes. Moreover, he suspected that the changes had been made for ideological reasons by someone working in the newspaper who disagreed with him. I agreed that the incident, as he described it, seemed both uncivil and journalistically unforgivable, but then I enquired further into the nature of the changes, which as I recall related to the expression of some clearly unfashionable view, with which Desmond is well endowed.

On hearing what the changes were, I immediately saw what had occurred. I explained to Desmond that what he had described was not, as he suspected, an incident of ideological sabotage. It was simply the newspaper exercising its editorial judgment in an instance where one of its contributors had been observed to be wrong. But, he protested, the change related not to an issue of fact but a matter of opinion. He had simply stated something which he, on the basis of the analysis he was outlining, believed to be true. That is as may be, I replied, but it was still wrong. What had occurred, I guessed, was that a senior editor or sub-editor, on reading his piece, had realised that one of Dr Fennell's beliefs was actually incorrect, and had altered it to save embarrassment to both the author and the newspaper. There was no ideological agenda, no conspiracy, no lack of civility. On the contrary, the change had been made to protect Desmond Fennell from the consequences of his own error. He could hardly argue, I pointed out, that a newspaper was not entitled to prevent wrongheaded views getting into its columns. The fact that what he had written was his sincerely-held opinion based on several decades of contemplation and observation was neither here nor there – he was as wrong as if he had carelessly alluded to Christmas Day falling on June 23rd.

Unfortunately, Desmond Fennell's work is littered with such errors. For example, his book, *Heresy: The Battle of Ideas in Modern Ireland*, even before it begins, carries the dedication: 'To Bernadette McAliskey with respect'. This is almost certainly a mistake. If such a dedication were to be attached to an article for a national newspaper in Ireland, it is absolutely certain that it would have to be removed to protect the author's credibility. Clearly, if he had been thinking correctly, he would not have written such a thing. He is, after all, an educated man. What could he be thinking of? To associate himself with a woman who is herself not merely wrong about everything, but even dangerously wrong, was surely an act of extreme foolishness. But it doesn't stop there: on the very next page is reproduced a quotation: 'One loves the freedom of men because one loves men. There is therefore a deep humanism in every true Nationalist.' The author of the statement was Pádraig Pearse. Clearly, again, both the sentiment and the choice of it are ill-advised. Desmond Fennell obviously does not know that nationalism is not something that right-thinking people should have to read about other than in a pejorative connotation, and the same goes for Pádraig Pearse. If such a quotation were to appear in a newspaper article, it would cause those who run the newspaper to have hurried consultations concerning the wisdom of having people like Desmond Fennell write any further articles. But perhaps if the reference could be deleted and Dr Fennell were to make no protest about the excision, there might exist some hope for his rehabilitation

Growing up and into the ferment of ideological debate that has provided the intellectual infrastructure of what is termed Modern Ireland, it was difficult to know precisely what to do about Desmond Fennell. On the one hand, he was clearly a deeply reactionary individual, a man with what appeared to be a benign interest in the welfare of Catholicism, nationalism and other elements that had been placed in the loading bay awaiting removal from the premises. While the rest of us were busily tying up the boxes and moving the skip into place, Desmond Fennell was moving obliviously through the boxes, reopening them, pulling out their contents and making notes. Occasionally, he would pause and make a statement or ask a question. 'Have women souls?' he would ask, puffing on his pipe. 'Get up the yard, Desmond, and get out of the way till we clear out this stuff,' we would reply, and he would smile and take to his rummaging afresh.

There was something deeply disquieting about Desmond Fennell and his smile and his pipe. What he was saying all along was that the reconstruction we were embarked upon was not necessarily well advised, not definitively justified, not unambiguously valorous or self-evidently correct. There were many others who said similar things, but virtually all of these others did not count by virtue of defect of intellect, fanaticism of heart or redness of neck. Such people bore only too obvious witness to their own error. But Fennell was different. He was, it seemed, quite an intelligent man. He did not speak like a redneck. He came, it was rumoured, from Belfast, and he had been to university in both Dublin and Bonn. He had travelled widely and had lived for extended periods in Spain, Germany, Sweden and the United States. He also appeared to lack all outward appearances of fanaticism. He spoke calmly, in structured sentences; he rarely lost his cool; and always there was the smile, as though he found the whole discussion faintly amusing but had nothing better to do at the moment than to join in.

Desmond Fennell's books, too, posed a grave difficulty. Usually, if a reactionary has written a book, it is merely a matter of obtaining a copy and using the contents to taunt or dismiss him. The problem with Desmond Fennell's books was that, once you had dug one of them out and perused it, you were left with the unsettling possibility that here was a man who, if he was right about anything, might be right about everything. The only thing to be done, therefore, was hide the book away, present a false account of its contents, and confine your analysis of Desmond Fennell to a satirical impersonation of him smoking his pipe.

The problem with Desmond Fennell, then, is not simply that he is wrong, but that he just does not appreciate how wrong he is. But there is an entirely different problem with Desmond Fennell's thinking: such is its complex inter-working and scrupulous attention to logic and progression, that if he turns out to be right about anything, he could well turn out to have been right about everything. It is therefore quite obvious why things he writes have to be altered: only by doing so can we protect ourselves from the appalling vista that he might one day turn out to have been right.

Desmond Fennell himself has always seemed oddly prepared to countenance the possibility that he was wrong, if not about everything then perhaps about any thing or anything. In one of the pieces reprinted in *Nice People and Rednecks*, he wrote:

> I am in the business of thinking about things and making my thoughts public. There may be some people who pursue this way of life, and who believe that by thinking seriously and carefully they can arrive at the full truth about something, and state that truth in a manner which makes its trueness self-evident to intelligent people. If there are such persons, I am not one of them.
>
> I am a prober and trier. I believe that, by thinking seriously and carefully about some matter, I can arrive at *something like* the truth about it – a first version of the truth, a trial version – and that there is a fair chance that this will seem true, or partly true, to some people. To progress beyond that, to get a better hold of the truth, to fill out my statement of it, and to make that statement more obviously true to some people, I need to place it in front of people and get their responses to it. (p. 126–7)

Now this kind of thing was deeply inconvenient. For Desmond Fennell to fit into his allocated slot in the public discourse, it was imperative that his statements and behaviour followed a particular pattern. As someone who was – as clearly he was – resistant to some modern ideas, it was imperative, for example, that he be intolerant, inflexible, dogmatic and entrenched in his views. That he appeared not to be these things, but on the contrary open and flexible and anxious to hear other viewpoints, was deeply disturbing. It was, after all, a central belief in the manifesto of the modernising tendency to which many of us had sworn allegiance that everyone opposed to it was gripped by a profound intolerance based on ignorance and fear of losing power. Desmond Fennell, puffing on his pipe and saying 'Let's have a good chin-wag about all this', was not behaving within his prescribed function. Moreover, the difficulty about responding to his invitation to talk was that he appeared to know what he was talking about, and was therefore in serious danger of winning the argument.

In some circles, this penny took a while to drop. There was a time, for example, when Desmond Fennell appeared regularly on Irish television. Then, one day, he ceased to do so. Observing him on and off, during the years when he was a regular participant in debates on both television and radio, I was struck by the dissonance between what was clearly his allocated role in these debates and his actual execution of that role.

What is often not understood about media debate concerning social and political issues in Ireland is that things are rarely as they seem. On the surface, debates about nationalism, abortion, unmarried mothers or whatever, appear to be authentic confrontations between opposing opinions, with the media operators as neutral conduits and facilitators. In fact, these discussion are mostly staged debates between those who are 'clearly right' and those who are 'manifestly wrong'. The purpose is not to ventilate an issue so as to enable the public to make up its mind, but rather to dramatise the confrontation between truth and error so that the public will become even more convinced of the truth. To this end, it is vital that those participating in public debate to defend what is 'manifestly wrong' must enter into a tacit agreement with their media hosts. This agreement incorporates a number of unstated but implicit conditions, viz.: thou shalt defend the indefensible (for example, clerical child abuse) by dint of dissembling or prevarication; thou shalt wear strange, old-fashioned clothing, whereby to signal an out-of-touchness with modern society; thou shalt become incoherent with rage in the course of the programme; and so forth.

In media terms, Fennell was what is thought of as an 'intelligent reactionary', which is to say that media operators immediately thought of his name when seeking to stage a debate between liberals and conservatives, modernisers or reactionaries. Since he clearly disagreed with or could puncture much of what liberals said, it followed that he sought to do so out of the only possible motivation for such dissent, which was, broadly, to do with a desire to prevent the forward march of Irish society and return us to the dark ages. The problem with Fennell was that, although agreeing to participate in such debates, he refused to behave in the prescribed manner. His dress was unexceptional. He did not wear tweed jackets or ostentatious emblems associated with derelict or outmoded belief systems. Worse, he insisted on seeking to shift the argument away from the tug-of-war between alleged liberalism and alleged conservatism and introduced alternative ways of seeing things. Occasionally, he would cause absolute consternation by agreeing with the liberal voices (this was especially dangerous when it occurred on the national broadcasting network, RTÉ, which had a statutory obligation to provide 'balance' in debates, an obligation clearly breached when a panel suddenly appeared to be unanimous on a particular subject).

I once asked Desmond Fennell why he no longer appeared on certain radio and television programmes, and he told me that he himself had decided to absent himself, as he had grown tired of being used as a whipping-boy to enable liberals to demonstrate their correctness. I believe he is wrong about this, too. Although he may, in fact, have turned down one or two invitations directly, it was his behaviour when participating, rather than his refusal to participate, that made his continued appearances untenable. It was only a matter of time before they stopped asking him anyway.

I don't want this to be misunderstood, or taken for ill will, but if I were Desmond Fennell, I might now have serious concerns about my prospect for earthly longevity. If it is true – and there is fairly widespread evidence to say that it is – that thinkers and artists are given enough time on this Earth to say what they have usefully to say, to complete, as it were, a coherent life-statement, and then move on, then Desmond Fennell may now, unless he has other errors up his sleeve, have completed his life's work.

His most recent book, *The Postwestern Condition: Between Chaos and Civilisation*, is, by any standards, an enviable legacy to bequeath at what may or may not prove to be the end of a long career in public thought. Reading through his earlier work – *Nice People and Rednecks*, his collection of short essays written mainly for the *Sunday Press*; his longer pieces, published in *Heresy*; or his critique of nationalism, *Beyond Nationalism: The Struggle Against Provinciality in the Modern World* – there is a strong sense of a search for coherence in the modern melee. In *The Postwestern Condition*, there is an overwhelming sense of discovery, of searching for among most of, perhaps all, the elements with which his life's work has grappled, albeit on the basis that there is no sense any longer to be found and that, moreover, this senselessness is the designed and required end of a process of civilisation that has unshackled itself from history, morality and restraint.

In *The Postwestern Condition*, Desmond Fennell argues that western civilisation, as we have always understood it, has ceased, without us knowing it, to exist. All of the values, principles and rules of behaviour, which have underpinned western art, politics, jurisprudence and morality, have been rendered obsolete, and been replaced by a different set of values, principles, rules and morals that owe nothing to coherence and everything to the rationalisation of what we term progress. This process, he argues, is enabled by the expansion of the money supply and the rolling affluence of western societies. He claims that the origins of this change are to be found in the bombing of Hiroshima and Nagasaki at the end of World War II, an action that so contravened existing western morality that it invited one of two responses: unequivocal condemnation throughout western society at such a deviation from what was previously thought right; or the deconstruction of those norms to make these events acceptable. Without anybody ever declaring this explicitly, the latter course was adopted.

The tacit endorsement of Hiroshima, in its acceptance of the savagery of the indiscriminate massacre of civilians, women and children, therefore, had legitimated the illegitimate, and in doing so amounted to the rejection of western civilisation and the initiation of a completely new civilisation, as yet inchoate but struggling to find its feet amongst the debris of the old. Thus, by Fennell's analysis, the influence of America in the modern world has brought to bear a completely new form of morality on world affairs, a morality by which certain things are justifiable even if they seem to be in conflict with previously accepted values and truths. Out of this, he argues, has developed a sprawling senselessness, which has spread to virtually every area of public thought in the societies over which American values have influence. He calls this place 'Amerope'. It is not yet, he says, a civilisation, but it certainly aspires to being one. He calls it 'a civilisation in the making'.

His thought-train takes him on an odyssey through the life of what we call the modern world, embracing gender politics, language, sexual liberation, media, masturbation, accommodation advertising, sitting down, and much, much, much more. He strips the senselessness down to its chassis and looks at its naked nonsense. It is, though in other ways a deeply frightening book, in this sense, reassuring for those who have been aware of this senselessness and imagined that they were simply going mad.

Out of this, Fennell fashions what, if it were to be his final contribution to the intellectual life of this planet, would be a sublime and clear-sighted statement of how he found us. I harp upon my sense of its possible finality, not because I believe its author to be incapable of further achievement, still less poised with one foot over the grave, but because, having read *The Postwestern Condition*, I am unable to imagine what Desmond Fennell has left himself to say. He follows the logic of his argument along its natural and inexorable course, observing as he goes. Fennell is not just an academic or a reporter, but an artist who writes the history of everyday society as it unfolds before his eyes, and not as a catalogue of facts but an illumination of meaning.

The Postwestern Condition is a taut, spare book, the text of which runs to just 115 pages. It is, in fact, a rewrite of a significantly longer book, *Uncertain Dawn: Hiroshima and the Beginning of Post-western Civilisation*, published a couple of years before, which Fennell revised because he felt it had not correctly identified the incomplete nature of the emerging civilisation. The precursor was written as a diary, compiled over a few months around his observations on an extended holiday in the United States in 1994, and the later book is a distillation of the most essential elements of those diaries, with a new set of conclusions.

The Postwestern Condition is not an easy book to read. It presumes a great deal of the knowledge, interest, zeal and curiosity of the reader. Almost every second sentence is both loaded and laden with layers of meaning. It has about it that density and precision that one associates with a George Steiner or a Camille Paglia, both of whom receive more than routine mentions in Fennell's work.

The Postwestern Condition can be read in isolation, but with the greatest difficulty. Ideally, it should be read as a postscript to the previous works of Desmond Fennell, a final summing-up for the benefit of a jury that has been paying close attention but which now requires to be told what the evidence means. If, in his previous works, Fennell has adduced evidence, from his own society and those he has visited throughout his long career as an academic and writer, in this he draws it together in terms of its significance for the entirety of mankind. Here, we see him finally tie together the strands of enquiry he had been observed to untangle in *Heresy* and *Nice People and Rednecks*. In the last piece in the latter book, he had framed, by way of summarising his own puzzlement with what he had been observing, this question: '... it is a matter of looking at this modern life as it is exemplified in Ireland, and of asking, in one domain after another: is that a fit life for man, a pro-human or anti-human arrangement, or the most intelligent way of organising things?' (p. 157)

(I am interested in Fennell's use of the word 'man'. Fennell is the kind of man who always uses the word 'man', when he means not just men but women as well. It is a tendency that leads his work to be revised in the early hours by sub-editors anxious to protect their newspaper, reading public and not least the author himself from the consequences of such flagrant error. He does it, I think, not because he is a pedant, although he is probably that as well, but because he knows that sounding like a pedant will aggravate certain people enough to think about him and what he is saying. I am interested in it, too, because of a growing awareness in me that Desmond Fennell's core theme is really the collapse of authority of the old kind, and its replacement with a form of authority that is untenable because it is founded on lies. Fennell belongs to the old authority, of classical civilisation, of what is termed patriarchal society, of western values based on Christian beliefs and teaching. And with his pipe in his mouth, this is precisely what he looks like, and precisely, too, why he gets up the noses of people to whom manliness is a red rag.)

What Desmond Fennell seemed to have in mind in that passage, and indeed in many of the pieces reproduced in that particular book, was something that had perplexed many of us in the latter part of the twentieth century: the development of a society in Ireland according to ideas with which Fennell had grappled all his life, ideas that did not appear to be coherent, but which emerged according to the exigencies of the moment and continued to remain long after they became untenable. When we wished to speak of the origins of these ideas, or the architects of the emerging society, we spoke of 'liberalism' or 'pseudo-liberalism', and 'liberals', 'secular-liberals' and 'Dublin 4 liberals'. Fennell, like others, had sought for many years to dig up the roots of these phenomena, to establish the precise nature of their core motivations and aspirations, but without more than modest success. Like many of us, he had been assuming that there must be some sense to all this, a coherence too complex or too sophisticated to be perceived by those who most found it worrisome. Now, in *The Postwestern Condition*, Fennell at last has traced the root to its point of origin, and discovered that there is nothing there but the black hole of amorality presented by Hiroshima. It is a bold and spectacular theory and it makes sense.

This is not a book about Ireland, or Russia, or America, or Germany, but about all of those places, and everywhere else as well. There are just four pages in the book that relate specifically to Ireland, and these to the removal of explicit references to God and Christianity from the Irish Constitution and other key documents relating to the belief systems of Irish society. This section, as though included to demonstrate that Ireland is no more and no less than another outpost of the creeping postwestern condition, provides a clue to the nature of Fennell's voyage from the start. One of the accusations levelled against him was that he was a parochialist, a reactionary nostalgic, yearning for and seeking to recreate the conditions of Ireland past. Nobody who read his books could possibly say this about him, but one does not expect one's critics to read one's books.

When someone like Desmond Fennell sticks his head up in modern Ireland, and keeps it there in the face of the aunt sally masquerading as an intellectual debate, it is imperative that the general public be precluded from perceiving that there might be anything sensible in what he says. There are many devices for achieving this, including distortion, personal invective, demonisation and censorship. The Postwestern Condition has not been widely read in Ireland, and this is for a range of reasons, some of which are undoubtedly to do with the dense and difficult nature of the thought. But without doubt also, the fact that many people who might have profited from reading this book have not done so, has to do with a concerted effort to close Fennell down, to depict him in an unfavourable, antiquated light. Few of the devices used to achieve this have been as blatant as the manner of the critical reviewing of The Postwestern Condition.

The Irish Times, for example, published a review of this book by a Bill McSweeney, described as a teacher in the International

Peace Studies programme of the Irish School of Ecumenics, that succeeded in avoiding any mention of the book's main theme. The bombing of Hiroshima is such a clear-cut theme of this book that, in advance of actually reading it, one's thoughts tend to drift as follows: 'What on Earth is Fennell on about now, and what can the events at Hiroshima, more than half-a-century ago, possibly have to do with it?' In other words, it is scarcely possible to pick up this book, flick through it casually and cast an eye over its blurb and Preface without comprehending that it is a book with the idea of Hiroshima at its centre, and to be sufficiently puzzled about this to investigate the logic of it. And yet, Bill McSweeney, writing in Ireland's leading quality newspaper, did not, in the course of an 800-word review, use the word 'Hiroshima' at all. He described Fennell as 'a fiery critic of modernism'; 'a serial contributor to the Letters page'; 'a staunch, if not always lucid, defender of his own personal take on the human condition'; 'an intellectual best described as a pamphleteer of the old school'; 'a moralist who inveighs against contemporary ills'; and in sundry other ways. McSweeney characterised *The Postwestern Condition* as a torrent of invective against moral chaos (as though there might be something wrong with this if it were true) and accused Fennell of offering 'little more than a litany of generalisations unsupported by any convincing evidence'. But at no time in his review did the reviewer either tell his readers what Fennell's book was actually about, or suggest that he was even aware of what the core subject was.

There are, it seems to me, just two possible conclusions: either the reviewer did not read the book at all, or he wished to withhold from his readers the most basic intelligence concerning Fennell's actual subject matter. If this was his intention, he succeeded admirably, presenting this latest book by Desmond Fennell as 'yet another' tiresome rant about the terrible nature of modern life. One is struck by the thought that if such people were really as convinced that Fennell is as wrong about everything as they would have us believe, they might at least outline fully the extent of his error, so that we could all have a good old belly laugh at his stupidity.

It is strange that Desmond Fennell's work appears to attract, in the most acute way, the full brunt of the conditions that he diagnoses. When he talks about the split that occurred in the western mind following Hiroshima, he is describing a kind of global dissociation, a severing of logic and emotion so as to justify the monstrous, something close to what T.S. Eliot called the 'dissociation of sensibility' in the modern condition. It is interesting to observe that the very disease that Fennell diagnosed is capable of producing unlimited amounts of the intellectual microbes required to keep the virus of sense at bay. The targets include, unsurprisingly, both Fennell and his analysis.

I recall watching a television debate in Ireland at the time of the publication of *Uncertain Dawn,* in which Desmond Fennell was pitted against an academic from one of the Dublin universities. Fennell was at a disadvantage in that the presenter, typically, had not read his book, but he was making reasonable headway in explaining himself and his ideas when, out of the blue, someone said something about unmarried mothers, and the epidemic of fatherlessness in the United States. Fennell elaborated on this crisis for a moment or two, outlining some of the social damage that resulted, particularly as it related to fatherless children. And then, with an almost audible gulp, the academic launched into a retort centred on the fact that his own father had died when he was a small child. 'Am I a leper?' he demanded. He was visibly shaking and almost dancing with rage. At this moment, *Uncertain Dawn* died an instant death in the public mind, a book so full of error that it had nearly made a grown-up orphan cry. The audience immediately rushed – all but literally – to the side of the bereaved academic. Desmond Fennell was dead in the water, the man who had tried to suggest that a poor innocent child, deprived of his father at an early age, was some sort of leper. There are, of course, ways of answering this kind of emotive nonsense: it is possible to make a very clear distinction, for example, between children who lose a parent by death and children who are deprived of a parent through the unexplained disappearance of that parent, or worse, the sense that the parent has voluntarily abandoned his child or children. Fennell did not seem minded to resort to such argument. He was probably right, for there is no place for logic in a cauldron of piety and emotion. Such is the nature of intellectual debate in modern Ireland.

Ireland has essentially just three kinds of writers: one, those who focus on the local to the exclusion of everything else; two, those who focus, for precisely the converse reasons, on everything else to the exclusion of the local; and those who seek in Irish life and society an illustration of the universal, both to illuminate the local and better comprehend the universal. In this final category, Desmond Fennell is perhaps alone among his contemporaries.

He is great indeed. What sets him apart is that he set out willing to be wrong, to cast his eye over Irish society and try to make sense of it, not of itself, but of its place in a greater order. And what he has discovered, finally, is not its place in a greater order but in perhaps the greatest disorder the planet has ever seen.

No. Desmond Fennell is not a reactionary, nor a nostalgic, still less a parochialist. No, and as he says, he is against fixed ideas; he wants us to think long and hard about where it is we want to go, the better to get there in good shape and remain there in safety. If he harps upon the past it is not that he desires to return there, but that he demands of those leading us elsewhere that they say where it is they propose to take us, and how they think we are going to live when we arrive. Desmond Fennell, far from wishing to remain, merely wants to be reassured so that he can be first upon the bus on the morning of departure, smoking his pipe and smiling at the latecomers before leading them astray with the error of his ways.

FAITH, FATHERLAND AND MOTHER TONGUE

Nollaig Ó Gadhra

FAITH, FATHERLAND and mother tongue are three themes that have occupied a great deal of Desmond Fennell's writing over the years. In this essay, I intend to illustrate how they were at the heart of what motivated Fennell in what were, for me in any case, the two most important inputs he had into Irish life. These were the *Iosrael in Iarchonnacht* movement and the attempt to forge a way forward for the problems of Ulster.

There is a strong religious dimension to much of Fennell's work, not only because he recognises the importance of religion as a cementing factor in the life of communities, but also because he sees religious belief and practice as an essential part of the cultural as well as the spiritual heritage of people and communities, as natural as the air we breathe or the landscape people inhabit, and to be ignored at our peril if we wish to have any rational debate or comprehensive consideration of problems and possible solutions.

Hence, the resurrection of the Israeli state and the Hebrew language were, I think, subjects that were important to Fennell's exploration of the world. They formed part of his contribution to the challenge of getting down seriously to saving the Gaeltacht, which he outlined in his essay 'Language Revival: is it already a lost cause?' in the *Irish Times* on 21 January 1969, part of a special supplement to mark the 50th anniversary of the founding of Dáil Éireann.

Douglas Gageby, editor of the *Irish Times* in the sixties, allowed Fennell – the 'hermit' who had taken himself off to Iarchonnacht a few years before, to work out his future salvation – to spell it out for the nation, and the huge Irish-language establishment of 'Gaelic circles' around the Dublin Government at the time: if the aim of an '*Éire Ghaelach*' was to mean anything, it meant ordinary Irish people living in ordinary communities where Irish was the everyday language, where most services were available in the national language, and where all the areas of modern technology, media, crafts and learning were being developed and fostered and marketed in the modern world in the same way that the Dutch, the Danes, the Swedes, the Greeks, and the Finlanders do.

Fennell stated, correctly and bluntly, that the only place this was a reality to some degree, or had any likelihood of being achieved in the immediate future, was in the surviving traditional Gaeltacht communities. That is, in north-west Donegal, north-west Mayo, in a small part of west Kerry, but most of all in what he came to popularise in the public mind as 'Iarchonnacht' – that fairly extensive area (larger than County Louth) west of Lough Corrib in County Galway, plus the offshore Aran Islands where Irish was still the predominant community language. The language continued to live here in spite of all sorts of difficulties, including government neglect, economic under-development, emigration, and an increasing influx of new life-styles and technologies through the medium of English that were rapidly replacing the traditional crafts, skills and occupations.

Fennell, in my view, shook the political and indeed the language establishment to its foundations with his call to attention. And to action. He did so by his sharp and persistently provocative pursuit of the facts, by the bald expression in cold print of just how bad things were in 'Gaelic Ireland' at the time, and by proposing initiatives and structures of government and administration that would improve things; that would 'develop' rather than 'save' the Gaeltacht, but which also had a lesson for *all* neglected and declining communities in Ireland, be they in far-flung 'congested' but English-speaking areas, in many cases further from the capital than the *Gaeltachtaí*, or in inner-city areas in Dublin and Belfast.

This 'new departure' on the fiftieth anniversary of the Irish Declaration of Independence took off for a while in a new debate about 'Saving the West', a 'Federal Ireland', with all that this implied for Ulster, and *Cearta Sibhialta na Gaeltachta*, which ran an important General Election candidate in West Galway in June 1969, thus raising the profile of the Gaeltacht and its problems further.

In all this, Desmond Fennell, then living in Maoinis, Carna, on the western edge of the 'New Israel' he was proposing, played a constructive part. He wrote and re-wrote pamphlets, articles and slogans. He spoke, lectured and preached from every possible platform – from provincial papers who were normally hostile to anybody who questioned their own 'Save the West' orthodoxy, to RTÉ radio and television, whenever the season was right. In so doing, Fennell was accused by some as 'sitting on the fence', of encouraging the locals, or some of them at least, to do all the hard work, crafting out the snowballs that were to be thrown by others at lay and clerical, political and community establishments. That was not my recollection of the period. And I say that as one of those who had, as an RTÉ producer, covered Fennell's campaign in both languages and was partially inspired by the 'events of '69' to move west as part of an ongoing anti-metropolitan trend that ended in very different ways for a range of very different people from Casla to California.

The idea of a Gaeltacht local radio to serve Iarchonnacht was one of the ideas Fennell had proposed and which *Cearta Sibhialta* had put into their election manifesto. The idea of 'doing it ourselves', rather than waiting for state action, arose in the autumn of 1969, based partially on what had been achieved in Derry by the Bogside residents during the siege of that community in August, and led to the pirate 'Saor-Raidió Chonamara' the following Easter, and the state-sponsored offical Raidió na Gaeltachta in Easter 1972. The symbolism of giving the Gaeltacht its first ever authentic voice on the new radio technology on Easter Sunday had its own symbolism too, and was inspired in a way by Mr Fennell's supportive comments during those years in the excellent radio column that he used to write for the *Irish Press*.

It should be noted, however, that what Fennell proposed was a local radio station for Iarchonnacht, and, by extension, the other Gaeltacht communities. I am not aware that he ever spelled out the importance or nature of the relationship there should be between the different Gaeltacht services, from the top of Donegal to the lush pastures of Ráth Cairn, Contae na Mí. And while presumably he had no objection to Raidió na Gaeltachta being made available on VHF, or whatever new technologies were coming along at the time, to Irish speakers all over the country, including Gaeltacht families in Dublin who still used Irish or had an interest in things 'back home', he was very opposed to any attempt to take Raidió na Gaeltachta out of the hands of the local Gaeltacht communities, either by unionised 'professional broadcasters' or political and other elites who wanted to vest all radio infrastructure and growth in

RTÉ. The fact that some of the locals took quick crash-courses of 'work-experience' in Dublin and then used this to install themselves as the new know-all elites in rival unions (some British based!) as soon as it became clear that there would be a scramble for *'jabanna maithe sa mbaile'*, is only one of the ironic developments down the road that surprised many people.

It is no more ironic than the fact that Mr Fennell, living in Maoinis, availed of his radio column in English in the De Valera newspaper group, widely read in the Gaeltacht, and indeed of all sorts of Dublin-based and frequently 'west British' media to promote his Gaeltacht crusade. But this was absolutely necessary. One of Desmond Fennell's major achievements in those years was to change the way Irish people, in government and politics, in religion and educational establishments, even in the GAA and the Irish language organisations, but most especially in the mainstream 'Irish' media, looked at the Gaeltacht, the 'language revival', and by extension the way we all govern ourselves locally and regionally.

The *Iosrael in Iarhonnacht* challenge was not the only form of excellent journalistic crusading in which Desmond Fennell engaged. Ever since he used to write a blunt and abrupt but usually thought-provoking column in Irish, 'Gan Fiacail', in the *Sunday Press* in the 1950s, Desmond Fennell has always been playing with ideas, asking sharp but necessary questions and trying to engage in dialogue with people in any language or from any background. This crusading journalism had developed into 'Fennell on Sunday' a decade later – yet another reminder of just how crucial to the mainstream of Irish debate and dialogue the Press group was up to the 1990s.

Desmond was still settled in Iarchonnacht, where there was no fax, e-mail had yet to be invented, and you could barely hear the telephone message if, as sometimes happened, the *Sunday Press* did not get its copy on time in the post. I seem to recall on a number of occasions, when Desmond's weekly sermon did not make the *Sunday Press*, the greatest disappointment was from Northern nationalists and republicans, and from friends 'from the other tradition', who were fascinated by the man who always had the courage to stand up for his 'own people', by which they meant those of the nationalist/Catholic tradition in the North.

There also seems to have been some sort of arrangement that if Desmond did not make the *Sunday Press*, his column would be offered to the daily *Irish Press* where editor Tim Pat Coogan usually published it as an opinion/feature article. I can remember the different reaction of the different 'market'. Especially people who did not notice the name of the author as they rapidly glanced down the features page on a busy Monday morning. The most frequent comment was, 'why don't they publish more good features like this in the mainstream dailies?' – before realising that it was only the Fennell column with a wider middle page spread, and possibly a few photographs, but with no picture of the author.

Let me add, by the way of balance, as they say, that at a personal level, while I always enjoyed Desmond Fennell's powerful writing, his amazing courage in tackling issues in religion, politics or culture, and the sheer depth, diversity and ongoing excitement of his exploration of the world, he could also be a difficult person to work with. But even those of us who worked with him on some projects were sorry that he took a less active role in others (e.g. the campaign against Section 31 or the whole terrible nightmare of prisoners' rights). Yet we could always rely on him for personal encouragement, for advice and for genuine insights about other ways to carry on a cause.

It would be a pity if a lot of this work by Fennell in the campaigning and journalistic area was neglected while we try to make sense out of some of his more complex religious, cultural and philosophical work. As one reads back over some of this latter material, one finds that there are a number of key ideas that Desmond pursued and which he re-wrote or summarised in book form – in order to keep them before the public? That is why the relative lack of weight that Irish thinkers and media persons in general give to the Fennell writings is all the more mysterious. It is almost as if Fennell was effectively 'phased out' from the generality of Irish media debate.

I mentioned earlier the strong religious dimension to Desmond Fennell's work. *The Changing Face of Catholic Ireland*, which was edited by Fennell, and based substantially on his work and commentary as an editor of *Herder Correspondence* (from the autumn of 1964 to January 1968), is one of his finest contributions in this regard. His work with *Herder*, being effectively the mainspring behind the international English-language edition of a firmly-established German theological magazine, was unique in timing (the heydays of the Second Vatican Council and after) but also in location. For it was a Dublin-based, English-language, Catholic publication being edited by a multi-lingual Gael, who already had walked a lot of different European countries as well as south-east Asia, and America, but was particularly familiar with the genuine culture of post-World War II (West) Germany, and the problems that the re-industrialisation of the Adenauer era had presented.

Now, in the mid-1960s, you had this Dub of Belfast background trying to relay the impact of Vatican II and the new EEC industrial society back to Ireland and to the wider Catholic Church, which owed so much to the Irish throughout the English-speaking world. You also had Fennell, the man who had seen the 'new' Sweden and all the models of modern urban 'socialised' society in northern and western Europe in particular, and had made up his own independent mind about the flaws and the faults a full decade and a half before most of the rest of us got into the act of comparing things at home 'with the rest of Europe'.

Fennell is obviously thinking it out for himself in much of this *Herder* material, and while his postscript at the end entitled 'The Mind of Catholic Ireland' obviously stands the test of time and context, for those who want to understand and allow for such things, the crunch, for me in any case, comes in Chapter 13, which asks: 'How Irish is Irish Catholicism?'

This is a transcript of a television debate in RTÉ, broadcast on 15 January 1967 and chaired by Seán Mac Réamoinn, who had covered all four sessions of Vatican II with distinction for the national broadcaster. Taking part in the discussion about the nature of Irish Catholicism were Fr Thomas McInerney OP, Professor of Fundamental Theology at a Dominican House of Studies near Dublin, Kevin B. Nowlan, Associate Professor of Modern Irish History in UCD, and Desmond Fennell, then editor of *Herder Correspondence*.

Towards the end of what was probably an edited television half an hour of debate, Fennell suggests:

> But even on the most pragmatic of levels, surely what makes a culture or a religion Irish or German or French is the inheritance of a continuous heritage of hundreds and hundreds of years of a particular form of that religion or culture in the one country; and certainly any Irish Catholic who goes to the Continent finds out that he belongs to an extremely rootless Catholic life. He goes to Germany or he goes to Spain or he goes to the Tyrol and he finds people still celebrating the saints of their forefathers, indeed praying much more to Irish saints, as I have noticed myself in central Europe, than they do in Ireland. (p. 184)

Here again we note the personal experience of the man who
had walked the ground 'in Europe' long before most others of
his generation. Earlier in the debate (p. 179) he spells out his
view on the key issue in a way those who currently waffle
regularly in the Irish media about a 'Celtic Church', with scant
attention either to genuine Irish history or tight definitions,
could usefully reflect upon. Referring to an article in *Herder
Correspondence* in November 1966 about Irish-American
Catholic scholarships at that time, Fennell said:

> The article dealt with the discussion of Irish Catholicism
> that has been going on among American Catholics over
> the past few years and criticized some insular and almost
> racial ideas which had crept into that discussion. But
> what we want to talk about tonight is how we, ourselves,
> have fallen into the same errors in the debate about, and
> public criticism of, Irish Catholicism which has been
> going on for the past few years in Ireland. We have been
> finding lots of things wrong, and rightly so, but we
> haven't really been getting at the root of what is wrong
> because we have been seeing far too many things that are
> part of he cultural history of Western Europe or part of
> the Church in all of Western Europe – we have been
> seeing these things as specifically Irish. For instance, we
> have been complaining that various devotions of minor
> importance have pushed Christ and the Mass to one side.
> Now, of course, they are complaining about this in every
> country in Western Europe at the moment and, in fact,
> these devotions which have taken the place of the
> eucharist or of the Mass are mostly of French and Italian
> and, in general, Continental origin. They did not arise in
> this country.... We have complained about our
> squeamishness in relation to sexual things, about our

idea that sin is almost equivalent to sexual sin but, of course, these have been prevalent in every country in Europe, in the Protestant cultures and the Catholic cultures in the nineteenth and twentieth centuries, and to an extreme degree in the English-speaking world. After all, our modern Catholicism was formed in the era we call Victorian. Briefly, I throw open for the discussion the thesis, the statement, that what we call Irish Catholicism is simply the fusion of nineteenth-century Victorian culture with the thing that came from Rome to this country in the nineteenth century, the thing that came from the Continent. That's all we have, that's what we call Irish Catholicism.

If I had to give Fennell, the philosopher, a label, I would probably call him a 'particularist', i.e. a person who in politics and economics, whatever about administration and industrial or personnel relations, tries to tell it as it is, sets out problems in some kind of context most can understand, and then prescribes the bones of a definition or a 'solution' without all the details. That said, it is clear from the essay, as it is from the entire book, that the exercise itself greatly affected Fennell himself – forcing him to think deeply about Irish society, the Irish nation with its various definitions, and the whole complex mix of Irish culture, language and tradition. Desmond realised, when he really got down to it, that 'frank' statements of an 'extreme' nature from no-nonsense writers like Pearse and MacNeill, as well as Beckett and Joyce, but most especially from that decent Church of Ireland son of a rural Connacht clergyman, Douglas Hyde, were nothing short of the truth. It was Hyde, after all, who once said he founded the Gaelic League 'to continue to ensure that Ireland would remain an interesting country to live in.'

Fennell rightly points out the failure to fully achieve this *aisling*, even if it helped to bring down not only the British

Empire but the whole process of western colonial rule in the process throughout the twentieth century. But he clearly admits that the war is not over yet, and that the search for a new solution or at least for a fresh departure, must come from a profound and tightly-defined re-evaluation of history in context. The type of thing Seán de Fréine did in 1960 with *Saoirse Gan Só*, later translated into English as *The Great Silence*.

In that regard it may be worth quoting what Desmond wrote in the postscript to *The Changing Face of Catholic Ireland* (p. 190) about the ongoing identity problem that Vatican II created for Irish Catholicism and for Irish academic and theological study and debate in particular. He says:

> As a result, there was no view available of Irish Catholic life as it was, though this was not realized. Naturally, people wanted and needed to know things and to say things about themselves as members of the group that defined them and about the life they shared together. So they looked at one or other of the abstracted elements — or at combinations of them — linked them somehow with 'Irishness' or 'Catholicism' or with both together, and imagined that they were looking at and talking about themselves. Statements about 'the Irish', 'life in Ireland', 'Irish Catholicism', 'the Church' and 'Ireland' were not lacking. But they bore no direct relationship to reality. Their degree of insight was that of newspapers, old-style catechisms, nationalist rhetoric, positivistic learning, public-house eloquence and adolescents' dreams.
>
> This blindness to ourselves was common to all, but its continuance must be laid squarely at the door of our learned academics: it was no accident that the most profound and comprehensive view of us published in

English in the last forty years — Seán de Fréine's *The Great Silence* – was not the work of a professor or even of a graduate. Whether located in theological seminaries or in institutions actually called 'universities', the University as such failed to fulfil its fundamental role as the ordinary source of general light and comprehensive vision.

Fennell took up where de Fréine left off (at least for the time being!) and went on to formulate his own theory of what the Irish rebellion was or should be all about, 50 years on, in *Cuireadh Chun na Triú Réabhlóide*, which was published in *Comhar* in 1965, as part of the lead-in to the commemoration of the 50th anniversary of 1916 by the monthly journal of An Comhchaidreamh, an inter-university Irish language organisation that had founded Gael-Linn a dozen years previously. I happened to be Uachtarán an Chomhchaidrimh that year and as part of our annual Gaeltacht Conference in 1966, we invited Mr Fennell to lecture in Tír an Fhia, Conamara, probably the most neglected but also probably the most predominantly Irish-speaking community in the country at that time.

I would like to think that this memorable *comhdháil* was one of the factors that persuaded Fennell to throw in his lot with the people of the 'integral Irish tradition', though it is also clear (e.g. from the interview with Carrie Crowley on RTÉ Radio's *Snapshots* programme) that there were other factors that led to the decisions to settle in Maoinis. It is clear, however, that at this stage in the mid-60s, Fennell had mixed feelings, not to mention doubts about the first, never mind the third revolution. See his 'The Failure of the Irish Revolution – and it's Success' in the *Capuchin Annual* in 1964. After honouring 1916 'appropriately' Desmond and family took off to Maoinis.

There follows a period, indeed years of hard work, deep thought, campaigning, pamphleteering, research in cooperation with others and indeed on his own, for Fennell, as he made an attempt towards peace and reconciliation based on the reality of the problems at the heart of the Ulster conflict. This is a massive legacy that would be impossible to summarise, but which will have to be put into the public record if ever we are to have a true account of the way some members of the Northern community, or those who spring from them, tried to listen openly to the case of all other sides, in secret and publicly, mainly without reward or recognition, in an attempt to move things in the right direction.

Years before most of the 'peacemakers', Mr Fennell would talk to *everybody*, at least for a while, but they, in turn, would have to listen to him! Of course, the 'liberal' media took Fennell to bits on occasion, but then they did the same thing twenty years later when John Hume first entered into dialogue with Gerry Adams...

The best summary of the development and the evolution of Fennell's thinking on all this 'Northern' business can be found, thankfully, in *Beyond Nationalism*. It is a complex and evolving work that literally reflects the thinking of a man in action, grappling with the tragedy of his country and his people, and that hints at an evolution of understanding as well as an evolution of possible solutions. In all this, however, even Fennell's critics must concede that his basic approach to the North has had a consistency of sorts that has indeed already had profound implications for serious Irish historians.

In a nutshell, it would seem that Fennell's basic thesis is that by any of the normal standards of nationhood, in western Europe at least, the Republic of Ireland's claim to full island-wide territorial integrity was ill-judged once it became clear that the Catholic/nationalist majority, the descendants of the historic Gaelic nation, were not prepared to stand up and fight, or at least patrol and police, those areas of Ulster-Scots and

Protestant colonisation in north-east Ulster. He fully accepted that these 'Loyalist' people were more loyal to their own cultural legacy than even the Crown, but this should present no problems for a real reconciliation with Catholic neighbours within a proper federal system. The majority passion of insisting that the British-orientated people of the North were 'fellow Irishmen', came from the Wolfe Tone doctrine of French revolutionary republicanism in a centralised unicultural state. This idealistic aim of 'uniting all Irishmen', without either consulting most of them or recognising their very diverse backgrounds and cultural identities, had not only failed in most revolutionary efforts since the eighteenth century, but allowed the colonial master an advantage in the 'divide and conquer' area, as well as letting builders of a 'New Ireland', 'Young Ireland', any future sort of Ireland, off the hook when it came to spelling out what they wanted to happen in the Ireland of their future dreams.

It was for this reason that the Gaelic League and the post-1916 Sinn Féin that evolved through people who had been 'at school to the Gaelic League' were, in Fennell's estimation, the only real effort to make Ireland a nation once again since the defeats at Kinsale, Aughrim and the Boyne. And it was no coincidence that it was the 1916–1919 generation of republican revolutionary Sinn Féiners who did most to allow Ireland take its place amongst the nations in the twentieth century, and set an example for the entire 'Third World' at the same time.

The real trouble with the Irish Revolution, according to Fennell, was that we failed to finish it. Or that, after the deaths of such diverse thinkers as Michael Collins and Liam Mellows (who had a common basic outlook according to the signficant essay Desmond wrote for the Sinn Féin booklet *An Aisling* to mark the 60th anniversary of the Easter Rising in 1976) we failed to develop fresh thinking in the bitterness of the Civil

War and the stagnation of Free State politics. This was heightened by the betrayal of the Northern 'new minority', who were thrown to the tender mercies of Stormont and the Orange Order in return for 'peace', or at least order and comfort south of the border. It was Fennell's basic point, a full generation ago, that the pro-British people in Ulster were entitled to recognition and to some sort of federal structure that would defend their rights and identity while living beside their Irish neighbours. But he also insisted that, at the same time, some sort of joint authority, and equal recognition of their identity, would have to be given to the Catholic/Gaelic nation throughout all of Ulster, and which had been deliberately persecuted since partition.

Fennell, it is clear, had a huge influence on Provisional Sinn Féin political thinking at an early stage. People like Ruairí Ó Brádaigh and the late Daithí Ó Conaill took some of his ideas on board from the outset, which is one of the reasons why other Irish political groups, in true Irish begrudger fashion, had nothing to do with them for years, even though they knew they were only common sense or at least deserved to be thrashed out in debate. This was not true for many of the Loyalists however, who recognised Fennell's *bona fides* each time he insisted to nationalist audiences or readers that the Ulster-Scots and British in north-east Ireland had rights that also needed to be reflected fairly in the structures under which they lived. Hence Fennell had dialogue with unionist Sammy Smith, shot by his own side in 1974 because he dared to travel to the Galway RTC 'Open Forum' to dialogue with a Southern 'Catholic' audience, and even more interesting, private debate with Major Bunting and Desmond Boal, Paisley's legal right hand man at the time.

Desmond Fennell, independent as ever, made his own contribution to the New Ireland Forum in 1984. But he seems to have decided about that time that he had said all he could say and would have to wait for some more favourable circumstances to run with his ideas, once we all evolved from the dark days of the 1980s that started with H-Blocks and economic depression and continued under the shadow of Reagan, Thatcher and FitzGerald. I am not aware of the advice, if any, Mr Fennell gave to Government or indeed to Mr Haughey in those years, nor is it clear to what extent Fennell's ideas were even allowed to be debated in *An Phoblacht/Republican News* as soon as both papers were merged and a new republican leadership dumped most of the hard creative work on federalism and federal solutions that had been done in conjunction with the Sinn Féin leadership of the previous decade. It should, however, be noted that people with no republican background whatsoever, like the late Dr Tom Barrington of the IPA, Tom Cullivan of the NCEA and the late Dioraí Ó Coirbhin, Secretary/Bursar of UCG, had also put a lot of effort into promoting a fresh start in Irish local government, even through a Society for the Advancement of Self-Government.

It would also appear, on the face of what has happened in Irish politics North and South in the last twenty years, that the Irish people are not really enthusiastic 'federalists' in the Fennell or continental European meaning of the word. The 'solution' to most problems that come along, be it bad roads, pollution control or health and safety regulations, nearly always seems to be an option for a 'new national agency', rather than a local alternative. It would be interesting to hear an update from Mr Fennell on this.

In his recent RTÉ interview with Carrie Crowley, Desmond Fennell said that almost everything he suggested or proposed for the Gaeltacht community of Iarchonnacht had been achieved – apart from a self-governing local structure in what would presumably and ideally be a federal Ireland as well. This is true in one sense, if you recall that the area, which had no local radio in 1969, now has a television network centre as well. There are 'outreach' branches of UCG in two centres, better roads (believe it or not!), much improved housing (but who can afford it?), fleets of big cars, but still a disgraceful public transport service. There is a lot of employment over a wider spectrum, at least in the thirty-mile coastal stretch west of Galway city. More local people are staying and are in fairly well-paid employment. Most women are now working outside the home. There are far fewer children and a corresponding decline in family and community solidarity. Iarchonnacht will shortly be faced with the horrendous 'problems' of more older people living longer while both members of the family in the next generation are out at work in an era of increasing 'individualisation'. This is not simply a tax and income and lifestyle matter. It even has implications for the language itself and the passing on of the cultural and religious heritage from generation to generation. One item in Desmond's 1969 shopping list, which thankfully did not materialise, was 'Ireland's first atomic power station'. *Is olc an ghaoth!* It only shows how perceptions of what is 'modern' change too.

In suggesting in 1969 that even the 'real' Gaeltacht had no more than fifteen years to live, it is clear that Fennell was probably trying to 'frighten' bureaucracy and others into urgent action. He was wrong of course, even allowing for his update, 'The Last Years of the Gaeltacht', in the *Crane Bag* in 1981. This was a particularly pessimistic essay at a time when, it seems to me, Fennell was already giving up on the Iarchonnacht chapter of his life.

I am less familiar with his work from the mid-1980s to the mid-1990s, but that said, I find *The Postwestern Condition: Between Chaos and Civilisation*, which was published in 1999, a fascinating if short work that paints a broad picture of history and philosophy that is probably all the better because Desmond is less involved personally in the mechanics and the politics of what is involved. This is vintage Fennell, placing us all, and himself, at the centre of the world as we try to work out, together, the great mysteries and problems of society, and of humanity.

My only real regret is that Fennell's latest book seems to have got less attention here in Ireland than even some of his earlier work, and that badly needs revision, or at least re-assessment. Even on the Iarchonnacht business it seems to me he needs to re-assess, in his cold, no-nonsense way, what succeeded and why. What were the factors he either ignored or underestimated? In what way did his own rather narrow criticism of other Gaelic and cooperative efforts of good-will blind him to the wider picture of Iarchonnacht, in the Gaeltacht and in Ireland in general? Everything from the reality that nearly all Gaeltacht kids now go to third level, and as bilinguals or trilinguals have no hang-ups about 'the Irish leaving us poor', or the various subtle cultural insults to which Irish unilingual children used to be subject, even from their 'republican' neighbours! Then there is the whole world of the Internet, long distance learning, Raidió na Gaeltachta on the Astra Satellite, so that we now have more subscribers for certain types of services in Irish off the island of Ireland than at home. Gaeltacht teenagers travel the world with an ease that one could not even imagine in 1969. The phones are better also. Cheap and regular telephone stories of life, love and family now cross the Atlantic on a daily basis and in a developing and vivid dialect that is light years away from those stilted formal letters in school-acquired English that were the main legacy of contact between Conamara in Boston and Conamara at home for a century after the Famine.

I would be the last to suggest that we are out of the woods yet. The Irish language and its associated heritages are in grave danger still, primarily because of numbers. There are too many people all over the globe, and even in the Gaeltacht, who are not particularly concerned about passing on what they have, and what entitles them to a notch in world history, to the next generation. Or they seem to think that, like the poor, these things will always be with us, without special conscious efforts and planned action. Worse still, the language is being undermined not only by the regular bombardment of English, or should I say American, in a society that is no longer being Anglicised to the extent that it is being Americanised into a sort of fifty-first state on the other side of the Atlantic. But also because some, perhaps most people and groups, are no longer being required to take the trouble to either learn or use correctly the full flow of genuine vernacular Irish, which we used to hear on Raidió na Gaeltachta when it opened for example.

Given that Fennell suggested in his original Iarchonnacht call to action in 1969 that we should aim at making the Gaeltacht communities 'representative community segments of modern Irish life' there is, I suggest, lots of work that Desmond Fennell still needs to do. He should not be allowed to hang up his boots or his pen just yet, and if this humble contribution outlining some of his achievements and reminding all of us how mean we have been in recognising his achievements helps in any way to put Fennell into print more frequently at home, then I will be glad. I will even suggest that those who are concerned with historical spin-doctoring should make a real effort at revision of the record at a weekend seminar or summer school – in Iarchonnacht of course! The collapse of the 'left' and the almost total acceptance by Irish trade unions, the Labour Party and even the RTÉ commentators, of the stock-market culture of 'privatisation' and 'competition' as a solution for economic ills, in areas as diverse as health insurance, oil refining, broadcasting, and even the provision of cleaning and meal services in hospitals, in the post-Berlin Wall era, is another area in which Fennell with his familiarity with German culture has a lot to offer us. As indeed he would have if somebody were wise enough to ask him to look at our post Nice referendum situation.

Rumours have it that on a recent visit back to Maoinis, Mr Fennell showed an interest in purchasing a grave in that exotic location. Which given the complexities of these matters under the current bureaucratic systems is an acceptable manifestation of foresight as well as a manifestation of belief in *toil Dé!* Ach is *maith le Dia cabhair,* and communities no more than individuals like to think *gur gaire cabhair Dé ná an doras!*

Desmond Fennell has made an interesting and unique contribution to Irish life in the second half of the twentieth century. *Ach níl a sheal caite ná baol air!* Like the Irish language, which was first outlawed by the Statutes of Kilkenny in 1367, Desmond will be around for a long time yet, stimulating, cajoling, annoying us, but most of all inspiring us into action for causes that we know are good, because they are human, even humane. But also because there is a need and an urgency with most of them and nobody but *sinn féin amháin* (or should that be *muid féin – or muidne?*) will undertake them. *Go bhfeicfear an síol faoi bhláth!*

'THE CANON OF IRISH HISTORY – A CHALLENGE' RECONSIDERED[1]

J.J. LEE

DESMOND FENNELL'S 'Against Revisionism' remains among the handful of articles on 'revisionism' still worth engaging with. Published originally in 1988, and in revised form in 1989, it was reprinted in the collection edited by Ciaran Brady, *Interpreting Irish History: The Debate on Historical Revisionism 1938-1994* (Dublin, 1994). Despite my difficulty with its central proposition, it deserves regular reflection as an incisive statement on the purpose of historical inquiry, reminding us yet again that there is no substitute for a first class mind.

This essay can only be a preliminary contribution to engaging with the issues raised by Fennell. I'm conscious that my concentration on the central proposition, that the proper type of history writing is that 'which sustains, energises and bonds a nation, and thus serves its well-being' (Brady, p. 187), does nothing like justice to the texture of Fennell's thinking, and involves neglect of several arresting insights. I too am highly sceptical of 'revisionism', as an ideological project, as distinct from proper scholarly revisionism as an integral feature of historical enquiry. But I am sceptical for different reasons from Desmond Fennell. For it seems to me his argument can be used against 'anti-revisionism' as logically as against 'revisionism', and it then becomes merely a matter of ideological taste which 'bonding' one prefers. Of course Desmond Fennell also exhorts the historian to strive for truth. My problem is how can one combine this with an equally firm conviction that the truth must serve a particular ideological purpose? It seems to me that the two objectives are mutually incompatible.

I cleave to a different view in principle. This is the conviction that confronting the truth about one's collective identity, whatever it may be, is as necessary, if as purgative, a duty as facing the truth about one's individual identity. Acknowledging flaws in one's collective character need no more tend to self-destruction, as Desmond Fennell fears, than acknowledging flaws in one's personal character necessarily leads to self-destruction. It all depends on one's response to the discovery.

Of course, just as none of us is ever anxious to face the full truth about ourselves utterly unflinchingly, neither are we likely to constantly confront our collective identity in an unrelenting search for unvarnished truth. Nevertheless this has to be the ideal in principle, however impossible it may be of complete attainment, given the frailty of human nature. But it seems to me essential that one should always strive towards this ideal, even while conceding that one will never fully achieve it. Otherwise all historical writing is doomed to become inescapably the handmaiden of ideology. The historian then features as simply another form of propagandist, disguised even from oneself beneath the conventional garb of scholarship, citing one's sources, but in the end a poseur, for the conventions of scholarship have been used to sustain a predetermined conclusion.

It can be readily acknowledged that ample examples of this can be found in nineteenth and early twentieth century historical writing of an Irish nationalist as well as an Irish unionist/British imperialist persuasion. In comparative context, the Irish nationalist writing may have been somewhat more moderate than might have been expected, but it was still recognisably a species of war history. The tone modulated somewhat following the political changes in 1921, and increasingly as the first generation of the *Irish Historical Studies* school came into prominence from roughly the late nineteen thirties. But this ethos then revived with a vengeance, partly in response to the unfolding conflict in Northern Ireland, when history once more came to be consciously summoned as a weapon in a current ideological conflict. Much of it reverted to being a variety of war propaganda, however draped in the decorous folds of scholarship.

If 'revisionism' be, as Fennell calls it, 'the historiography of the Irish counter-revolution' (Brady, p. 186), the 'counter-revolution' is driven by a sense of 'moral bonding' of its own. It is precisely this moral conviction that makes it blind to the unsatisfactory use of evidence which affects, for instance, much of the later work of a scholar of such unimpeachable integrity as F.S.L. Lyons. Where Fennell insists that he is 'not opposed to the writing of any kind of history, if its factual narrative is substantially true, and its interpretation, moral or otherwise clearly argued', but that he objects to revisionist history 'being accepted as the proper or true history of modern Ireland' (Brady, p. 187), he raises the spectre of the historian rejecting a 'substantially true' factual account on ideological grounds. But can this not cut in any direction, leaving interpretation to depend largely on the ideological whim of the writer?

I have great difficulty conceiving of a history which is factually correct serving a cause contrary to the public welfare of any mature people, except possibly at a moment of supreme national danger, as say in Britain in 1940,when it may have been deemed untimely to undermine some cherished self-image. Where the real problem with 'revisionism' (and pre- or anti- 'revisionism' alike) arises at a professional level is where it is not 'substantially true'. It is one of the sadder features of the intellectual history of the past generation that the standards of the use of evidence set in the first generation of the *Irish Historical Studies* school lapsed so lamentably. For the fundamental issue is that which the founders of *Irish Historical Studies* had striven so strenuously to confront, the scholarly use of evidence. It is only when work is subjected to serious scholarly critique that its validity can be ascertained. Until the 'well-being of the nation' is served by truth, warts and all, there will be something rotten at the heart of any nation – or of any other cause – that requires false history to sustain it.

But truth in this regard can be tested only by the case-study technique. Far too much of the 'revisionist' debate has confined itself to generalities, with Irish nationalism/unionism/British nationalism/imperialism idolised, or demonised. It is only by detailed critique of text after text that one can come to close quarters with the issues. The case-study I have selected here is frequently cited as a core revisionist text. That is the celebrated article by Rev. Professor Francis Shaw SJ, 'The Canon of Irish history – a Challenge'.

The painful parturition of this article has been frequently recited. Father Shaw submitted it in response to an invitation to contribute to the Spring 1966 issue of *Studies* commemorating the Easter Rising. But the editor rejected it on the grounds that 'a critical study of this kind might be thought to be untimely and even inappropriate in what was, in effect, a commemorative issue' (Editor, 'Foreword', *Studies*, Summer

1972, p. 113). Father Shaw revised it by August 1966, and it is that version which *Studies* published in 1972.

Father Shaw died in 1970. The editor introduced the article with an explicitly propagandistic purpose with reference to the conflict in Northern Ireland. The editorial refers to the IRA 'interpretation of Ireland's patriotic past' and 'the fears of the other side' as both myths, using myth, not in the anthropological sense, but as simple falsehood. 'Neither set of false beliefs can bring anything other than latent or open violence and destruction to this country' (p. 114). The editor does not provide evidence as to why either set of beliefs is necessarily 'false'. It is simply stated as a self-evident truth. But much though one might wish it were true, that has to be demonstrated by the scholarly use of evidence. Assertion, even with the best will in the world, is not evidence. But this editorial gloss also can lead to a misunderstanding of Father Shaw's own purpose, as the editor himself concedes (p. 113). For Father Shaw, however much he might have agreed with the editor, was not writing under the shadow of the troubles in Northern Ireland. His article has very little on Irish nationalist-unionist relations in Northern Ireland at all.

What then is Father Shaw really about in the essay? His opening paragraph reads: 'In the right corner virgin Éire, virtuous and oppressed, in the left the Bloody Saxon, the unique source of every Irish ill and malaise; round eight, the duration of each round a hundred years: This might be said to be the accepted *mise en scène* of the Rising of Easter Week, and it may be added that the seconds in the English corner are usually degenerate Irish men. It is a straight story of black and white, of good "guys" and bad. The truth, of course, is different; there are many qualifications and complexities and this essay is concerned with some of them.'

Anyone proposing to substitute 'qualifications and

complexities' for 'black and white', is likely to appeal to the historian. As one of the arguments of this paper is that scholars should declare their own convictions, I can immediately identify with this desire. As long ago as 1965, I invoked Hugh Kearney's observation that '"Ireland" and "England" have been seen almost as human beings, instead of complex, articulated societies.'[2] When the proponent is a scholar as respected for his meticulous accuracy as Father Shaw, one is particularly hopeful of a measured, genuinely historical critique (Editor, p. 113).

Unfortunately, Father Shaw's text does not live up to his own admirable injunction. Despite some acute observations, his account itself becomes a thing of 'black and white'. By the end there are no complexities, simply a reversal of good guys and bad guys. But these are not mainly English and Irish. After his opening scene, the English vanish until the epilogue, over thirty pages later. In between, Father Shaw's main concern is to denounce the insurrectionary tradition in Irish nationalism, and to rehabilitate the reputation of the alleged 'degenerate Irishmen'.

The key to understanding Father Shaw's interpretation is the clause in his graphic opening paragraph, ostensibly an afterthought, but in fact the core of his argument, 'and it may be added that the seconds in the English corner are usually degenerate Irishmen.' It is the reputation of these 'degenerate Irishmen' that Father Shaw is determined to rehabilitate.

His real theme begins with the third paragraph. 'The canon of history of which I speak stamps the generation of 1916 as nationally degenerate, a generation in need of redemption by the shedding of blood. It honours one group of Irish men by denying honour to others whose merit is not less. In effect it teaches that only the Fenians and the Separatists had the good of their country at heart, that all others were either deluded or in one degree or another, sold to the enemy. This canon moulds the broad course of Irish history to a narrow pre-conceived pattern; it tells a story which is false and without foundation. It asks us to praise in others what we do not esteem or accept in ourselves. It condemns as being anti-Irish all who did not profess extremist nationalist doctrine... in the commonly accepted view of Irish history the Irishman of today is asked to disown his own past. He is expected to censure as unpatriotic the common Irishmen who were not attracted by the new revolutionary ideas, but who adhered to an ancient tradition. Irishmen of today are invited, at least implicitly, to apologise for their fellow countrymen who accepted loyally the serious guidance of the Church to which they belonged. Irishmen of today must despise as unmanly those of their own countrymen who preferred to solve problems, if possible, by peaceful rather than by violent means.' (p. 118)

Here the commitment of Father Shaw, rather than Professor Shaw, leaps at one through his praise of those 'who accepted loyally the serious guidance of the Church to which they belonged.' His core criticism of the canonical interpretation is that it is not sufficiently Catholic.

Father Shaw knows what 'the common Irishman' felt and wanted: 'It is high time that the common Irishman should come again into his own; it was he in any case who always bore the brunt of the struggle. The business of revolution was usually an Anglo-Irish affair; it flourished principally in the Pale' (p. 119). Although there is a somewhat more positive later reference to the Anglo-Irish (p. 152), 'the common Irishman' does not include them, or apparently the Pale in general or, it transpires, Dublin itself. Father Shaw's hero is Eoin MacNeill, 'the Antrim country-man', who in 1916 'warned Pearse, the Dublin city-man, that Dublin and Ireland were not the same, and he told Connolly that he could see no further than the city roof-tops' (p. 119).

Father Shaw goes further. The Citizen Army led by James Connolly 'can be omitted' from his essay 'because basically it is more a part of world history than of Irish history' (p. 119). What does this mean? Is Ireland somehow outside world history? Why should the two be mutually exclusive? Does Father Shaw cherish some image of 'true' Irish history out of which distasteful elements can be excluded? Many of the main influences in Irish history, as in the history of most other countries, are imported. To be consistent, he should have ignored republicanism, which he repeatedly describes as 'alien', but that does not prevent him from devoting most of his essay to it. The image of England and Ireland in opposite corners has begun to fade away by this stage. Father Shaw writes as a protagonist of Catholic Ireland, and of rural Ireland, against not only the rebels of 1916, but the Anglo-Irish, the Pale, Dublin, and the Citizen Army. And the logic of Father Shaw's preference for 'the Antrim country-man' over 'the Dublin city-man' (although MacNeill had lived in Dublin most of his life) suggests that the Belfast Protestant was doubly removed from his image of 'the common Irishman'.

The main reason Father Shaw advances for ignoring the Citizen Army is that Connolly mistakenly believed that the ancient Gaelic mode of life had been socialist and democratic. This seems a somewhat curious reason. By the same criteria he should have ignored Pearse, whose image of Gaelic Ireland was quite as unhistorical as Connolly's. Instead he devotes several pages to demonstrating how unhistorical his image of Gaelic Ireland was, instead of dismissing him as unworthy of any further critique.

Father Shaw concludes that 'the action of Easter Week as seen in retrospect over a half century stands in stark isolation. It had no strong link with the past: It was universally condemned by contemporaries: and the ideals which inspired it have not worn well; they have been quietly but firmly sidestepped by the Irish people: They are ideals which are proclaimed on the understanding that they remain as such' (p. 120).

All these statements may be valid. But they have to be debated. They cannot be simply proclaimed as if they were revealed truth. What does 'no strong link with the past' mean? Does it mean that there was no tradition of rebellion against British control of Ireland? Or does it mean that the majority of the Irish people did not want independence, and that they therefore rejected the idea of rebellion for independence in principle, as distinct from holding it to be impracticable in practice? This needs to be elaborated.

'It was universally condemned by contemporaries' is a pardonable misunderstanding by someone who took at face value the formal public condemnations and failed to examine contemporary comment at the level of source criticism normally deemed necessary for sound scholarship – although here it is only fair to say that specialists on the period had not conducted the necessary search either and that even thirty-five years later a good deal more remains to be done.[3] Father Shaw praises P.S. O'Hegarty's description of the Rising, 'universally and explosively unpopular', as 'courageously frank' (p. 149). But the question is not whether it is frank or not. It is whether it is correct or not.

Father Shaw concludes that 'The whole scene was changed by the barbarity of the executions and a little later by the threat of conscription. The Irish might at times be pro-British but the English never understood that deep down in every (or nearly every) Irishman there was an ancient, quiet, deep and natural understanding that Irishmen were different, that they were a people with a history and a distinctive way of life: that they were in fact a nation...'. Whether this be valid or not, it hardly seems to include the majority of unionists in his image of the 'Irishman'.

'The ideals which inspired it have not worn well'. What were these ideals? The Proclamation of the Republic guaranteed 'religious and civil liberty, equal rights and equal opportunities to all its citizens', extolling 'the happiness and prosperity of the whole nation and of all its parts, cherishing all the children of the nation equally, and oblivious of the differences carefully fostered by an alien Government which have divided a minority from the majority in the past.' The government of an independent Ireland was to be 'representative of the whole people of Ireland and elected by the suffrages of all her men and women'.

Which of these ideals had not worn well by 1966? In the most concrete case, Father Shaw overlooks how revolutionary the promise of full adult franchise was for the poorest men and for all women, who didn't have the vote. But then he insists that Ireland was a democracy already (p. 146). He provides no definition of democracy. It would normally seem to require at least two conditions: firstly, that every adult has the vote, and secondly, that that vote determines the government. Neither condition existed in the Ireland of 1916. At the very least Father Shaw's concept of democracy needs elaboration.

He is quite right to point out that the 'gallant allies in Europe' of the Proclamation, the Germans, 'have won no special relationship with the Irish people'. But he fails to point out that Pearse himself made the point at his trial that Germany mattered no more to him than England. The reference to 'gallant allies in Europe' was purely tactical.

This raises a recurring problem in assessing Father Shaw's critique of 'the political philosophy of Pearse'. However perceptive some of his comments, it is surprising how little he tries to contextualise Pearse's statements, particularly as he rightly observes that 'in the course of his life Pearse's political views changed considerably; in the last three or four years of his life the rate of change accelerated rapidly' (p. 121). It is as if he reads every word written by Pearse as an ultimate philosophical statement, which does not require locating in its historical context. The issue is basic to the use of evidence.

Father Shaw duly notes that 'in 1912 Pearse spoke in favour of Home Rule at a public meeting in O'Connell St., Dublin' (p. 121). The next sentence is that 'Soon after that he became a wholehearted separatist'. Shaw here employs the standard language of Irish political discourse. 'Wholehearted separatism' means simply independence in standard European political vocabulary, 'that dream of becoming a normal European nation' as Fennell puts it, succinctly but lethally, demolishing the assumption that there was something abnormal about it (Brady, p. 185). But then it has always been one of Fennell's strengths that he brings a much wider European perspective to bear on Irish experience than the traditionally limited horizons of much of Irish historiography, itself moulded within the assumptions and the language of the more powerful English culture.

Let us deconstruct the assumptions behind Father Shaw's sentences. One implies that Pearse had not been 'a wholehearted separatist' in 1912. But there was no reason why 'a wholehearted separatist' should not support the Home Rule Bill in 1912 if he felt it could be used to achieve independence. That was exactly what Pearse said quite straightforwardly at the time.

'In the last years of his life he became impatient with all who did not share his extremist views'. What was the extremism of his views? Was it that he wanted independence? Is Father Shaw saying that this was not the objective of the majority of the Irish people at the time? Perhaps it wasn't. But he produces no evidence. If he means by 'extremist views' the belief that the objective could only be achieved by rebellion, he is probably correct. If he means that a rebellion should be attempted now, then he is certainly correct.

Whatever he means by extremism, the concept needs elaboration. The implication is that it is identical with rebellion. But this had nothing to do with the issue of public attitudes to political violence in principle. The Irish who volunteered for service in the First World War were clearly not opposed to the idea of violence to secure political objectives. If Irish nationalists opposed rebellion in Ireland, it cannot have been because they opposed violence in principle. Was it then because they rejected the idea of independence for Ireland? Given that John Redmond's recruitment speeches heavily stress their potential contribution to securing Home Rule, widely interpreted to mean as much independence as possible, this seems highly improbable.

Or was the reluctance to rebel rather based on the assumption that, given the disparity in the command of violence between Britain and Ireland, rebellion was hopeless, and it therefore made no sense? This would actually accord with Father Shaw's citation from John Redmond to the effect that 'resistance to the Act of Union will always remain for us, as long as that Act lasts, a sacred duty; and the methods of resistance will remain for us merely a question of expediency. Resistance by force of arms would be absolutely justifiable if it were possible' (p. 147).

The issue here was not the morality, but the practicality, of rebellion. But the issue is also with Father Shaw's organisation of his material. For this quotation occurs twenty six pages later, and he fails to address its implications for his own positing of a fundamental difference in principle, as distinct from a contingent difference of tactics, between non-violent resistance and rebellion, in the public mind. The issue at least deserves debate rather than assertion as self-evident truth.

Father Shaw's views on Ulster Unionists are not entirely clear. Although his image of his ideal Ireland does not seem to instinctively have a place for them, he criticises the Rising because 'in 1916 it must have been apparent that separation from England could only divide the nation more deeply. Even the most modest measure of Home Rule for the whole country was wholly unacceptable to the Carson-led Ulstermen. In 1914 an armed soldiery stood between Ireland and its destiny; but that body was not the British army; it was the Ulster Volunteers. Logically the Rising of 1916 should have been in Belfast, and it should have been directed against those who illegally and by the use of force opposed the acceptance by the Irish people of the considerable degree of self-determination for thirty-two counties which was being offered to them' (p. 122).

This is a striking passage. Father Shaw seems to be saying that separation – i.e. independence in the normal European sense — 'could only divide the nation more deeply.' But if he is right to observe that 'the most modest measure of Home Rule for the whole country was wholly unacceptable to the Carson-led Ulstermen', it is difficult to see what can be 'more deeply' than 'wholly unacceptable'. Again the matter can be debated – but not within Father Shaw's term of reference here.

Note too that 'the most modest measure of Home Rule' of this sentence becomes two sentences later a 'considerable degree of self-determination'. Rarely can the terms of a Bill have been revised so rapidly. He wants on the one hand to condemn the 'Ulstermen' for rejecting so 'modest' a proposal, while simultaneously praising Redmond for achieving 'a considerable degree of self-determination'.

This is not the only example of disingenuousness. For in reality both the 'Ulstermen' and the British army opposed Irish independence. By using the evasive phrase that it wasn't the British army that 'stood between Ireland and its destiny', Father Shaw is able to avoid spelling out just what he felt that 'destiny' to be, and incidentally avoid the issue of the role of English policy in forging the framework within which Irish discourse was moulded. If Britain did not oppose independence, as distinct from Home Rule, it is difficult to see why the British army should have crushed the Rising, or Britain resisted subsequent attempts to achieve more than Home Rule.

The paragraph concludes with the comment that 'both the Irish Republican Brotherhood and the Volunteers were pledged to avoid any action which would cause disunity. On the fall of the dice which was cast in 1916 there were different possibilities, but amongst them the unity of Ireland did not figure.' But the phrase about the IRB and the Volunteers being pledged 'to avoid any action which would cause disunity' is, I fear, also self-delusive. The mere aspiration towards Irish independence was by definition divisive. Only by dissolving themselves could they fulfil this pledge in the face of unionist resistance.

Behind this type of argument there lurks something deeper in Father Shaw's psyche. It transpires that what he finds really repulsive about Pearse is 'the idea that patriotism and holiness are the same, that they are convertible concepts' (p. 122). Here it is once again the priest, Father Shaw, who is shocked by what is to him a form of blasphemy. He is all the more upset because Pearse purports to take Tone as his inspiration – and Father Shaw detests Tone, not least because of Tone's disdain for Catholicism in general and the clergy in particular (pp. 127-30). Indeed the 'Challenge' of his article has Tone as much as Pearse as the target. Probing though his individual comments can be, it is not unfair to say that Father Shaw is not only shocked at Tone and Pearse. He is scandalised by them.

His handling of the relationship between them raises its own difficulties. His observation that 'Pearse was not, for the most part, original' is based on the proposition that 'It is not difficult to discover the sources of Pearse's later political thinking. He makes it clear himself that he had nothing new to offer. He declares without qualification that on the subject of Irish nationalism everything that needed to be said had already been said' (p. 121). But Father Shaw does not seem to take full cognisance of the significance of his own observation that in fact 'Pearse did add two important themes'(p. 122). This should warn that everything Pearse said and did should be subjected to the usual scrutiny given to words and deeds, with each tested against the other. Father Shaw does scrutinise the words – or some words – of Pearse. But he tests them for their literal rendition of the sources he is using, not for Pearse's tactical purpose in using them.

Far from 'following' Tone, for instance, Pearse is using Tone, as he uses Christ, Colum Cille and Cú Chulainn, for his immediate purposes. Again Father Shaw fails to follow the import of his comment that Pearse observed Cú Chulainn may have never existed (p. 133), or that Pearse's idea of Cú Chulainn 'is almost entirely the fruit of his imagination', or of his important insight that 'by a fantastic flight of fancy he projected his own ideas into the vacuum of the past' (p. 131). Instead Father Shaw reverts to a scholarly but irrelevant exposition of the historical errors of Pearse's account. But the real historical question is not whether Pearse was factually correct about Cú Chulainn, any more than whether Connolly was factually correct about ancient Ireland. The historical question is why they choose to believe what they choose to believe about that Ireland. Pearse is not seeking to create his ideal modern Ireland in the image of Cú Chulainn. He is creating Cú Chulainn in the image of his ideal modern Ireland.

Where the inspiration for that modern Ireland comes from, why it is that ideal, and not some alternative one, he embraces, is the real historical question about Pearse, or indeed about the use he makes of his sources. In this regard, Shaw's approach is simultaneously scholarly in a textual sense and unscholarly in a historical sense.

It can indeed be argued that his whole treatment of Irish nationalism, for all his incidental insights, is itself unhistorical. He is repelled by the hatred for England motivating republicans in general and Pearse in particular. I'm not concerned here with how right he is about the motivation, although it is odd he fails to engage with Pearse's most explicit discussion of the meaning of hatred of England in an Irish context (*Political Writings and Speeches*, pp. 365-6). What is of concern is that he never stops to place the issue in comparative context. How does such hatred compare with the degree of hatred of the conquered for the conqueror in world history? How driven was Irish nationalism compared with other nationalisms by hatred for peoples other than their conquerors? How 'normal' or 'abnormal' was Irish nationalism in general, and republicanism in particular, in this regard?

Father Shaw devotes close attention to 'the old testament of Irish nationality', concluding that 'the Irish never subscribed to the conventional ideas of state and sovereignty, from which to some degree nationalism generally developed'. 'The idea of nation, one might say, came to them more naturally than that of state. They thought more of personal and local freedom, which they understood and prized, than they did of national freedom which they imperfectly appreciated' (p. 138).

This is a fascinating section. Once again, however, it is weakened by great vagueness about change over time, and by the almost complete absence of any comparative context. 'The old testament of Irish nationality' was not necessarily unrepresentative – of 'old testaments'. But the Irish, like most of the rest of mankind, changed their ideas over time. One could get the impression that Father Shaw believes that the old ideas are somehow authentic, in a way that the new ones are not. In fact they are both equally authentic or inauthentic for their circumstances.

Father Shaw's reflections on the role of political violence in Irish history deserve close scrutiny. Allegedly 'the notion of fighting for Ireland was not, and never had been familiar to the ordinary Irishman' (pp. 144-5). 'The Irishman fought for his religious beliefs, he fought for his home and land, and he fought for life itself or the food to sustain that life; but he did not belong to the world in which national sovereignty was maintained by the strength of standing armies' (pp. 144-5). He finds that 'Ireland's reaction to the threat of conscription during the First World War is full of significance; Irishmen by the thousand volunteered to fight in the British Army; in the Irish tradition that was a freeman's privilege; but to be compelled to fight for Britain was a different matter and was in fact judged to be incompatible with the Irishman's concept of nationhood' (p. 144). 'Two hundred thousand Irishmen might go voluntarily to fight with Britain but not twenty would go as conscripts' (p. 149).

Interesting an observation though this be, Father Shaw produces no supporting evidence. Recruitment in the First World War was lower in Ireland than in Britain. It was lower again in Catholic Ireland than in Protestant Ireland. The rejection of conscription came in 1918, when it can be presumed the vast majority of those who wished to fight were already in the army. It would have been really interesting to have seen the response if conscription had been imposed in 1914. The implication of Father Shaw's idea of how the Irish mind worked was that those who fought 'for Britain' voluntarily in 1914 would have rejected conscription. But the reasoning appears dubious. At the very least, would one not expect unionists to have responded positively to conscription? Despite his 'revisionism', Father Shaw just forgets unionists most of the time. Even apart from that, on what basis can one assert that only a handful of 'common Irishmen' would have joined in these circumstances? This needs close thought, not sweeping assertion. And who exactly did the Home Rule recruits of 1914 think they were fighting for: for Britain, or for Ireland, or for some blend of the two – or for neither of them, which would logically have been necessary for them to have conformed to the Father Shaw model? Describing them as fighting for a national sovereignty – any national sovereignty – is incompatible with his assertions about their idea of the state.

Father Shaw is outraged by the claim that the Rising 'saved Ireland's honour'. For him, the preceding generation did not require its honour to be saved because it had never been compromised. On the contrary, 'the people, it might be said, were moving always towards an ultimate goal of independence or self-determination, but at their own pace and in their own way' (p. 147). They weren't. They were moving at a pace and at a way determined by the dominant power in the country, which was British power, as fundamentally reflected in the normal presence of about 30,000 British troops in Ireland – a fact never alluded to by Father Shaw in his definition of 'democracy'.

'In 1916', he concludes, the Irish people generally had plainly chosen the broadly constitutional mode of attaining national objectives'. Pearse, on the contrary, 'one feels, would not have been satisfied to attain independence by peaceful means' (p. 149). But 'one feels' is not what historians normally consider satisfactory evidence. Here is what Pearse actually says in his penultimate pamphlet, *The Spiritual Nation*. 'Obviously if a nation can obtain its freedom without bloodshed, it is its duty so to obtain it. Those of us who believe that, in the circumstances of Ireland, it is not possible to obtain our freedom without bloodshed will admit this much. If England, after due pressure, were to say to us, "Here, take Ireland", no one would be so foolish as to answer, "No, we'd rather fight you for it". But things like that do not happen. One must fight, or at least be ready to fight' (*Political Writings and Speeches*, pp. 323-4). It is almost as if he is anticipating Father Shaw's 'feelings'.

Maybe Pearse was just being tactical again? Maybe. But the circumstances of composition lend particular weight to this pamphlet. In February 1916 Pearse was no longer writing as a feverish propagandist to convince doubters that a Rising must take place. The decision had by now been taken to rebel, and he no longer had to grasp at any straw that would reassure the doubters, either about a rebellion or about himself, given the earlier IRB suspicion of his credentials as a genuine rebel and not merely a cultural nationalist.

Father Shaw concludes that 'The Irish people did not become extremists or separatists overnight.' Here, although it is not very fair to Shaw to signal him out, when he is only repeating standard usage – no 'revisionist' in this respect – one must ask again how he defines 'extremist'? Does he mean it to be identical with separatist? Does 'extremist' refer to ends or means? If 'separatists' are 'extremists' because they desire independence, then one must ask how many Europeans are 'extremists', and for that matter what term one uses for those who not only aspire to independence for their own country but also aspire to deprive other countries of their independence? Are they 'extreme' extremists? Or does extremism mean a belief in the right to resistance against foreign occupation? If so, would not the volunteers for the First World War be 'extremists'? The question then would not be whether the Irish people were 'extremists' or not, but 'extremists' for what? This issue can be debated – but it must be debated. Genuine scholarly revisionism must interrogate all our assumptions about the past, not merely those we find convenient to criticise.

Here I confine myself to those which seem most relevant to the immediate argument. 'The Rising of 1916 was then a minority one, not only by reason of the ideas of the men who fought, but also by reason of the choice of physical force as a means. It is not an accident that Tone and O'Connell should have reacted so differently to what they had seen of the French Revolution. The thin stream which stretches from Tone through Mitchel and the Fenians is in fact not of the lifeblood of Irish nationhood. It is alien in origin and content, and in its choice of means: And it is worth recalling that it flourished as strongly on American as on Irish soil' (p. 150).

This is highly debateable. The earlier quotation from John Redmond suggests how contingent on circumstances rather than principle it may have been. Father Shaw fails to address the contention that for a majority the issue was not one of either/or, but of both/and. Nor does he ask why it should flourish in America, beyond implying this made it somehow deeply suspect in itself. He does not consider that it might be that America might provide a laboratory example of how the Irish at home might respond if living in a more democratic polity, where they were not repressed by the threat of overwhelming violence.

Father Shaw suggests that rebellion was 'alien'. He seems to imply that it was the French Revolution, or Republicanism, that somehow brought violence into Irish political life. This seems a bit odd given not only the massive English/British contribution to political violence in Ireland, but that the Irish were by no means incapable of perpetrating violence independently of British inspiration – only a few pages earlier he is extolling Irish fighting prowess in the, to him, benign context of the 'old testament' of Irish nationality.

Father Shaw concludes (p. 150) that 'the Revolution of 1916 was very much a fruit of the rise of nationalism, of extreme nationalism, and it was, too, set in a time in which war and martial triumph were in favour. Today the world is discarding extreme nationalism as a negative and divisive force and today the horror of warfare pursued to its logical end of total destruction has inclined men to view all warfare as barbarous.' There is certainly barbarism in all war. But Father Shaw is here overoptimistic. The 'extreme' nationalism of 1916 was the normal nationalism over much of Europe – perhaps even rather less 'extreme', depending on definitions, than that of many of the belligerents. It would be nice to think that mankind is coming 'to view all warfare as barbarous' as a result of the horrors of the twentieth century. But Father Shaw was writing this while the Vietnam War was raging, and as yet global demilitarisation hardly seems imminent.

He attributes three consequences to the Rising. The first is 'the wound of Partition'. But he admits that this was already highly likely. The second is the Civil War of 1922-3, although he himself claims no more than that it 'was a consequence, if not an inevitable one'. If it wasn't 'an inevitable one', then it can hardly be attributed directly to the Rising, although the argument would certainly be worth developing in detail. Strangely, he overlooks the War of Independence itself, arguably a more direct consequence. But these are foreplay, before he comes to the one that really rankles, and to which he gives far more subsequent attention.

'The third wound on the national unity, more often forgotten than the other two, will continue to fester until the injustice which causes it is removed. ... I refer to the many thousands of Irish men who fought and died bravely in the First World War and yet are virtually without honour in their own land.'

Father Shaw makes an interesting point here. The whole question of the Irish in the British army in the First World War certainly deserves more probing historical inquiry, and it is sad that it is the plaything of politics. Having denounced the insurrectionary tradition, and inveighed against 'violence', Father Shaw clearly has no sense of any incongruity between his denunciation of violence for political objectives and his veneration for the volunteers for the First World War. This was a courageous and timely call by Father Shaw, but it would have been interesting to have had him explore the logical consistency of his reasoning on the matter.

His peroration raises a host of wider issues. 'Ireland and Britain are two islands placed by God's creation beside one another. The paths of their respective histories have of necessity constantly crossed: in a sense they have always got in one another's way, and their relationship throughout the centuries has not been happy' (pp. 152-3). What does all this mean? 'God's creation' has placed nearly every country in the world beside some other one. 'The paths of their respective histories have of necessity constantly crossed'. The historical question is how have they crossed. 'Necessity' is a human concept. Who defines it? 'In a sense they have always got in one another's way'. What does this mean? In what sense, precisely? Always? Have they 'got in one another's way' equally? Again the issue here is not right or wrong, good or bad, etc. It is simply the historical record.

The fundamental fact about Anglo-Irish relations is not in fact that God put the two islands beside each other. It is the fundamental fact of the disparity in power between them – power as expressed through command of violence. Geography is important, but it does nothing on its own. It is permissive, not determinative. Power relations are the dynamic factor. The argument from geographical determinism evades the realities of history.

Father Shaw's conclusion is not only incongruous, but suffers from internal contradictions. Having gone to so much trouble to establish the 'true history' of Ireland to his satisfaction, he declares that 'In fact the events of 1916 and of the years which followed did close a chapter in a long history of strife, and it is time that we as a Christian people should forget the past. There can surely be no more criminal disservice to Ireland than the determination to keep the fire of hatred burning' (p. 153). But his whole argument hitherto has been that one should remember a true past and expunge a false one, indeed that remembering that true past is a precondition of peace in the present, as when he wants the sacrifice of those who died in the First World War remembered, or the wound 'will continue to fester'. And he certainly shrivels Irish history if he thinks that the only lesson of the past is 'the fire of hatred'. In his own version, that was not what Irish history was mainly about in any case.

It also flatly contradicts his fear of the future. The danger to Ireland in 1966 was not, he believes, Anglicisation, but one which 'threatens England equally with Ireland. It is the danger of the triumph of a common cosmopolitan vulgarity which threatens all cultural standards and the individuality of peoples everywhere' (p. 152). But as in his telling history is the main repository of 'the individuality of peoples', his prescription seems to run clean counter to his diagnosis.

Until his strange concluding paragraph Father Shaw seemed to me to share Desmond Fennell's view of the moral role of history. He is passionately proclaiming an image of his ideal Ireland based on an equally passionate commitment to moral bonding. He had a very definite view of Ireland, and of a distinctive Irish identity. Indeed, the weaknesses and contradictions of 'The Canon of Irish history' derived directly from his sense of moral bonding. Of course, it was a different moral bonding from the republican tradition. That, precisely, is the problem with the model. Once one knows the answer before one begins, once one knows the framework into which one will fit the evidence, then the evidence is not only seen, but selected, to fit the framework. One cannot keep an open mind on facts if proceeding from a closed mind on their interpretation.

There is no way for the historian, *qua* historian, to decide whether Father Shaw's moral bonding is any more or less desirable than Fennell's or any one else's. But there is a way to say whether it conforms more closely to the evidence or not, and only the historian is competent to say that. The only test for the historian is how far the use of evidence satisfies scholarly standards.

'The Canon of Irish history' is subordinated to a preordained end. For all its incidental insights, and its polemical power, it is that view that ultimately vitiates it as history, however stimulating as advocacy.

Father Shaw is reputed to have once dismissed the argument, 'Can't you keep to the facts' with the response 'Can't we leave the facts aside and keep to the argument' (Obituary of Fr Frank Shaw, *Irish Province News*, April 1971, p. 79). The issue is not basically one of where there is agreement on the facts but disagreement on their interpretation. On the contrary, ideologically driven historians, whether 'revisionist' or 'anti-revisionist' are so much prisoners of their passions that they select the facts to suit their case. That is why the issue as Fennell presents it does not seem to me to actually arise in the way they ply their craft most of the time. That too is why the close case-study of individual texts is a basic prerequisite for serious discussion of Irish history. I'm well aware that even taking the length I have to try to convey some of the issues involved in assessing Father Shaw still only skims the surface of much of his presentation, which in effect is an overview of Irish history. I'm also well aware that many of the points I make can be debated, just as I'm aware my essay has done full justice to neither Fennell nor Shaw.

It should however stimulate debate on an article which many have cited as if no further discussion were necessary. Only close textual criticism can rescue the standards of Irish historical scholarship from the ideologists. Of course this will make no impression on many, so wedded to their world-view as to be impervious to evidence. But it can at least provide the evidence to identify genuine scholarship. That in itself would be some progress towards a degree of intellectual and emotional maturity so patently lacking in much of 'revisionism'. This may be a Sisyphean endeavour, human nature being what it is. But however Sisyphean, it has to be fought for, in every generation, by those who believe that scholarship is a crucial component of a civilisation. The search for 'true history' revolves around constant debate. There could be no more stimulating debating companion than Desmond Fennell.

Notes

1.   My thanks to Prof Seán Ó Coileáin and Dr Seán Ua Súilleabháin of the Department of Irish, UCC, Niall Keogh, Department of History, UCC, and to Patricia Quigley, Jesuit Library, Milltown Park, for assistance on biographical material. They are in no way implicated in the use or misuse I have made of their generosity. Biographical details of Fr Shaw can be found in Pádraig Ó Snodaigh, 'Cúlra Impiriúil Fr Francis Shaw', *Comhar*, 48, 1, Eanáir 1989, p. 12; 'Francis Shaw', in Diarmuid Breathnach and Máire Ní Mhurchú, *Beathaisneis a trí, 1882-1982*, (Baile Átha Cliath, 1992), p. 152; *Irish Province News*, April 1971.

2.   H.F. Kearney, 'Mercantilism and Ireland', in T. Desmond Williams (ed.), *Historical Studies*, 1 (London, 1958), p. 66, quoted in J. Lee, 'An economic history of Irish railways, 1830-1853' (MA thesis, UCD, 1965), v.

3.   J.J. Lee, *Ireland 1912-1985* (Cambridge, 1990), pp. 28-36.

A PROTESTANT RESPONSE

RISTEÁRD Ó GLAISNE

I DON'T KNOW when I first met him, but my memories of him do go far back.

I was a country boy from West Cork, interested in people and ideas. He was one to two years younger than I was: he was born in Belfast in 1929. We were both university undergraduates. He was at University College Dublin, I was a Trinity man. He was head of An Cumann Liteartha in UCD for a while: he invited me to lecture there on one occasion. We were both speakers at an all-Ireland intervarsity debate in Trinity's Regent House one night in Irish. I don't think we ever talked together in any other language, then or since. He wrote for *Comhar*, the relatively enterprising monthly magazine in Irish. I liked his querying, questing style. He was Irish and international. Good.

When Hutchinsons of London brought out his first book, *Mainly in Wonder*, in 1959, I was surprised to learn that he was, as he chose to put it, 'of Catholic Irish country stock'.

'I was born in Belfast and grew up in Dublin, where my father was a wholesale grocer,' he said in the foreword. Well, that figured.

'By Irish standards I am a city man.' Yes, yes. He looked a bit of a city man to me. Somewhere along the line, I discovered that he had been educated in the O'Connell schools and in Belvedere College, that prestigious Jesuit institution in Dublin. 'But in the world I set out to see I was quickly made to understand that I was essentially a peasant...'. Now, he didn't look like a peasant to me – physically, sartorially, intellectually. However, part at least of what he had to say about being 'essentially a peasant' could make sense: 'My people had never developed a native urban civilization.' His father came from Sligo; in Dublin he started as a retail grocer. His mother came from Belfast.

I saw little or nothing of Deasún (Desmond) in the fifties, nor indeed very much of him from that on. But he was writing quite prolifically, and I followed with interest most of what he wrote and did.

I feel a sense of excitement as I draw towards me a bundle of books, pamphlets and articles by him. Fennell's writings over the years show a concern with the Irish scene, an interest in a very sizeable section of the world, and a consciousness of some of the major political, economic, social and philosophical forces bearing upon community life. Clearly he has read significantly and meditated upon life. He is multi-lingual. He is highly articulate. In speaking, he talks in an agreeable, sensibly modulated way. He has travelled widely. Good-looking, sophisticated, of easy, if slightly distant, carriage, he could (in different circumstances) have been made something of a guru for print, platform, radio and television. Something of a prophet.

He did appear more than willing to assume such a role. Why, then, has he not been made more of here in Ireland? My guess is that there have been various possible explanations. I think he has probably collided sometimes with others who are also ambitious to tell what we should be doing. There may be issues of principle, and temperament. Unfortunately, he manages to leave the impression amongst quite a few of those who turn in his direction (sometimes without his saying a word) that he is supercilious. And, of course, people can react negatively to his rebukes and criticisms, and often do: they feel threatened, or offended.

The writings I have of his are mostly in English – what he has written in Irish is surprisingly small, and, writing that, I am suddenly smitten by something very like anger. If Fennell arrogated to himself a right to lecture us on values, and not least, by implication, the value of the Irish language, actual or potential, then we deserved better than that from him. A worthy cause warrants more than twenty years' loyalty. Everyone knows surely that not to use in public ways a language intimately and justifiably loved, and now in grievous danger, is to abuse it. What chance can Irish have if not frequently used by those of us who know it? If Dr Fennell thinks it is worth taking on the *zeitgeist*, where the west and east and south argue things out, why decide that the Irish language is a lost cause? If he is prepared to act with relative courage on one hotly argued front, why act so abjectly on the other? I've read much of what he has written on the subject of Irish, I agree with much of his analysis, but I am not impressed by his apathy there.

I cast an eye over what I have brought together. I'll pick a few fairly, or very, solid or suggestive items.

From early on, Fennell was exploring the implications of what was being accepted by the majority of Roman Catholic nationalists in Ireland in the first couple of decades of the twentieth century. He seemed to think that he was proposing something novel. He wasn't, to those of us who had read Hyde, Connolly, MacSwiney, Pearse, all of whom he evoked. We knew that a spiritual – social and individual – revolution was what the economic and political revolutions were about.

Until some time in his late teens he was in general sentiment a typical Irish nationalist of the twentieth century. 'Having learned Gaelic well at school, I wrote it fluently and with pleasure, spoke it to as many people as I could, and hoped that one day everyone would be speaking it again,' he has written (*Beyond Nationalism*, 1985, p. 22). 'Because I loved the Gaelic language and the Catholic religion, and they were the two most distinctive elements of my people's culture, I was glad to see them honoured in the public life of the state. Remembering the long hard struggle which it had taken to bring us to where we were, I was proud of the achievement of my father's generation . . . Some day, I hoped, Ireland would be united and the long struggle brought thereby, at last, to a successful end.' But, he wrote (ibid., 23-4):

> I first became aware of 'nationalism' as an element in the life around me – and as something apart from myself and most people – when I became a student at UCD. 'Nationalists' believed that Ireland was by nature a 'nation' like other nations, and would therefore not constitute a satisfactory life – not be 'free', 'whole', 'itself' – until it was in actual fact *like other nations* and a *real nation*. The nationalist conception of a real nation seemed to be 'a historical, settled community of mankind, manifested by a distinctive language and culture and by a sovereign state coterminous with its historical territory'. Since Ireland was not such a state, and did not have a distinctive language or, apart from its Catholicism, a distinctive culture, the nationalists proclaimed the urgent need to remedy these deficiencies. ... All the inhabitants of Ireland formed a single Irish

Nation. Protestations to the contrary by Northern Unionists were due to their having been deluded by their landlords and big capitalists. If England got out of the North ... they would recognise their Irishness. ... Perhaps because of my close associations with Belfast, it never occurred to me that the Northern Unionists belonged to the same people as I did. I knew that they considered themselves British, did not want to be liberated, and were hostile both to my people and to Irish nationalism. ... Nor again, did I believe that an all-Ireland state, or a change from English to Gaelic speech – even if such an unlikely thing were to happen – would produce a decisive change in the quality of our lives. ... Observing that we Irish had lost our distinctive culture, and that our actual culture, from cooking and etiquette to laws and language was essentially English, I concluded that we were *not* a nation but simply a 'people'... I thought it was pointless to try to create another European nation ...

Now, to those of us who are Irish nationalists, that may appear shocking or regrettable or unrealistic, but not wholly absurd. It is, therefore, startling to read the sentence that follows immediately: 'Let me say straight away that I now regard that particular line of reasoning as virtually meaningless and somewhat comical.'

As he elaborated on that, I felt growingly that, for all the surface clarity with which he wrote, he was rather confused about nationalism. And there is nothing particularly new about student disenchantment: it is very often profoundly unreliable as a guide to a more constructive understanding.

Nationalism I would describe as a political concept that predicates belief in the constructive value of that cultural amalgam that we call a nation. I was, I felt, now up against a problem I sometimes find when dealing with Desmond Fennell's ideas – his proneness to overdefine or underdefine when supposedly seeking to arrive at an agreed understanding of the concept he is alluding to. Here I would cite his strangely preferential assumptions when he uses the word 'human' and the word 'liberal', employing one positively, the other negatively.

In the quotation I gave from *Beyond Nationalism* he, like many, did not make a distinction between 'nation' and 'state' – though the term 'nation-state' presumably suggests a possible distinction: he did say (p. 26) that Ireland was for nationalists 'not a proper nation-state and consequently not a proper nation.' The nation is in the first instance a cultural entity, the state a political entity. I would think that in a world where the political often damages and distorts but is an ever-present reality (whether doing well or ill), there is much to be said for the nation-state. The state has often been capable of both defending and creatively developing the cohering cultural presence I (by no means uniquely!) describe as a nation.

Now, for the Jew or the Christian who has read the Bible with any care at all, the long history of the Jewish nation is a living, vivid and often painful memory of a nation that for nearly 2,000 years, up to 1948, did not have a nation-state, and whose language up till then was treated more terribly than ours in many ways. Irish people with a strong sense of their own nationhood have an abiding sense of Ireland, a nation well known to the world and to us, in our vast diaspora as well as our few million on this island. Nationally conscious Jews and Irish are not unique in this respect, either.

I write as an Irish Protestant of Desmond Fennell's work. What I have seen in my lifetime usefully illumines what I believe are Fennell's crude simplicities. I have seen the evil effects of Protestant sectarianism and of Roman Catholic sectarianism, and of the beneficent effects of Protestants and Roman Catholics loving or appreciating one another. Negative sectionalism has tended to cultivate ignorance and fear and dislike or hatred. 'Big capitalists' have not helped. I can speak without equivocation of the pleasure it is for a Protestant like me to know and very frequently use Irish. I would not wish less for any of my fellow-Protestants. I am sorry that there is not a greater unity either in Ireland or in Northern Ireland, and I see no possible Christian reason for apologising about feeling that way. Freedom and wholeness is in most things relative, but not to be derided. Political accommodations are, by definition, subject to mutations – of many kinds. So are cultural phenomena.

So, as briefly as possible, I record basic reactions I would have to that catalogue I quoted from *Beyond Nationalism,* which, even if he subsequently repudiated it (or part of it), contains ideas which have quite frequently been bandied around in my time. And – *pace* Fennell – we Irish hardly need to 'create' a nation, from the ground up at least! There is a diversity and a unity in every living nation. I hope Desmond was wrong in believing that 'the era of nations was ending'. He may have been right, but undoubtedly it will be a poor thing if our vaunted progress does not take action to preserve and nourish positive national differences.

In his enjoyable Irish travel book *A Connacht Journey* (1987) he has Nollaig Ó Gadhra describing his, Fennell's, attitude to the Gaeltacht and the Irish language as 'negative and defeatist'. I'm afraid I should have to agree, and yet I do so with a lively memory of two or three very interesting efforts he made in that area. From 1968 he and his family lived in Conamara, and he identified directly with a Gaeltacht Civil Rights Movement there and with the enormously significant and successful move towards an all-Gaelic radio station. His disillusionment at the failure of his hopes for an Israel-type cohesion of effort on behalf of the language in Conamara was profound, but the failure was foreseeable, given the obvious complexity of the attempt to reinstate Irish, upon which he has often written knowledgeably – e.g. in his books, *The State of the Nation* (1983) and *Heresy: The Battle of Ideas in Modern Ireland* (1993).

That Irish may be allowed to die by the Irish people is possible. That Christianity and many other precious things may be allowed to pass from our world through sheer inanition is also possible. But we do not necessarily have to allow any such things to occur without taking creative steps to prevent that. I turn to a 1969 *Irish Times* article of his: 'Language Revival: Is it already a lost cause?'

> The failure to Gaelicise even a representative nucleus of Irish life is a failure to revive Irish in the only sense that matters. It is a failure to attain even the *minimum* aim of revival. Such being the case, we are now challenged to accept this as our *de facto* decision on the matter – or to react vigorously and effectively against it. To let matters slide is not merely cowardly: it is harmful for several reasons.
>
> In the first place, it is demoralising for a people to be continually failing without hope of success – or effective desire for success – in an aim which they have set themselves. Such a situation is not only profoundly discouraging: it is productive of hypocrisy and mental befuddlement. Secondly, a great deal of public policy, especially in education, but by no means only there, is directed – in intent at least – towards the revival of Irish. By failing to change this, while at the same time failing to revive Irish, we are wasting our resources and frustrating our youth in an irresponsible fashion.

That contains much truth; it also contains assumptions and assertions that need to be – and in the case of Fennell, should not need to be – challenged. For here we are dealing with a very difficult case. It is nothing short of astonishing that Desmond Fennell should be one of the many types creating the situation which he decries.

He himself has in the past written very effectively of the demoralisation of the Irish people – and before the more recent deeply disturbing manifestations of that in Church circles. He has rightly drawn attention to how derivative so much in Irish life (perhaps particularly in English-speaking Irish life) has become. In such circumstances, the persistent and effective promotion of the Irish language as a living entity in our lives is to me a cause of some surprise. As one who gives priority to Irish, I am forever being frustrated in ways that are really not necessary – but I can see how comparatively easily a very great deal might be set right quite rapidly even at this juncture. As it is, I reckon that I personally, living in Dublin, use Irish without major effort perhaps half of my time. As a writer, Irish as we use it today is a fine and flexible instrument, and redolent of us as English isn't. But if we feed defeatism, general capitulation is a real danger.

Dr Fennell's writings sometimes turned out to be those of an extremist. Take the very beginning of *Whatever You Say, Say Nothing: Why Seamus Heaney is No. 1* (1991). The opening lines of the foreword are: 'In Ireland we have the habit of leaving it to foreigners to write the books about our famous writers. Of the nine books which now exist about the work of our most famous contemporary poet, Seamus Heaney, only one, by Elmer Andrews of the University of Ulster, has been written (or edited) in Ireland.' I take it that the second sentence was factual; it requires only a moment's reflection to realise that the first sentence was not. If one could accept his first assumption it would at least make a point, but because one can't accept it, he devalues his standing immediately and quite unnecessarily.

His comments on the maxim chosen as a title for his disquisition are intriguing, but, sadly, instead of cultivating a larger understanding, they gradually invite the reader to narrow his (and Heaney's) vision unhelpfully. I would hazard a guess that it is not the negative possibilities in a view deriving from such a maxim, so stressed by Fennell, which subsequently caused Heaney to be made a Nobel laureate. Though it contains much that is interesting, taken as a whole the essay seems to me to mispresent Heaney's real position, and real achievement, rather gravely.

Again, to take a major argument that he develops in the second half of the essay, while I have no difficulty in accepting the idea that poets, like others, are influenced by affluence, and by fashion, I have every difficulty in accepting the more extreme conclusions on Heaney. The worldly-wise approach there I regard as far too sweeping. That what Heaney offered contained elements now up-market I can see, but I would need a lot of convincing to share Fennell's conviction that these have been sedulously promoted in his poetry to meet market demands rather than appearing very naturally from a process which, after all, should not be entirely unexpected in a contemporary poet emerging from Heaney's personal experiences.

It is possible in analyses like those indulged in by Fennell there to be too clever by half. He writes responsibly, anent Heaney, of a poet's possible social function but, not uncharacteristically, overplays his hand (pp. 34–36):

> The first blurb of a Heaney collection to describe his work as 'meditative' is that of *Station Island*. Since then

he has been consciously not speaking to us even to 'say
nothing' ...
        ... The kind of poetry which Heaney practises is a
product of the consumerist era.

I suspect that Desmond Fennell is – to an extent greater than
he would care to admit, maybe – a product of his upbringing,
life at home, life at school. Not least in religious formation. For
a long time the Roman Catholic Church has been criticised on
all sorts of counts by dissidents. That may initially have tended
to make a man like Fennell rather aggressively ideological. The
tendency in the upper echelons of the Roman Catholic Church
to speak and act frequently in absolutist ways with regard to
many areas of life often seemed to non-Roman Catholics, or ex-
Roman Catholics, or rationally dissenting Roman Catholics,
arrogant. But I would think that the Fennells of this world were
often positively comforted rather than discomfited by what
they saw as the predictability of dissidents.

Many people are, still, more ideologically inclined than they
would care to concede, but the general spirit of the time, weary
of the negative consequences of ideology in so many fields,
would deprecate it publicly. The tendency in ideologists to limit
and to distort is so obvious as to render it unpopular until
periods of crisis arise.

Fennell's fundamental seriousness of purpose and incipient
sense of the dramatic readily identify areas of crisis. This causes
him to resort to ideology more than many of his intelligence
would today, and to favour a style that is at times somewhat
oracular. I would opine that in this he sees himself, rather
flatteringly, as largely inoculating himself against falling victim
to current epidemics in ideas and manners. He – like so many
of us – would like to think of himself as capable of getting
above the seductions of temporary passions whipped up by the

manipulators in a consumerist society. But ideology is not an acceptable antidote.

Dr Fennell's ideology for me, writing ultimately from a Protestant position, is a stylish, and at some points persuasive, refurbishment of traditional highbrow Roman Catholicism. All that is best in such a position readily gains our respect, but overweening loyalty to it (conscious, or even possibly unconscious) gives rise to concern amongst people like me and amongst many others, quite unlike me, who have found themselves more and more opting for a sort of inchoate liberalism that will tolerate almost anything – which Desmond Fennell certainly will not. That is where he will most readily be accused of dogmatism.

But the words 'ideology' and 'dogmatism' raise deep questions. Christianity has been institutionalised to one degree or another over a period of two thousand years or so. It asserts sin as exercising a deeply corrosive influence. It insists that Christ came to save the world from sin. It is judged accordingly. Dogma is of the essence here, but how extensive should it be? I think we must keep very aware that ideology is no sufficient substitute for truth, the static for reality, the political for the ideal, authoritarianism for the still, small voice of life's creative totality. I think that many people will find themselves in the anomalous position of agreeing largely with Dr Fennell about the menace of consumerist capitalism and yet be quite unable to relate to what appears to be major inconsistencies in his *Weltanschauung*. How can he give out about consumerism and then in his own public persona allow Irish to die? This suggests to me an intellectual and emotional superficiality (for his writings show that he is not blind to the significance of Irish) hardly fitting in the wise man.

The later part of Desmond Fennell's life and writings show a leaning in the direction of more abstract and academic thought. Perhaps the conferring of a doctorate, or tentative preparation for receiving such, has this effect on some, and in 1991 he did receive a doctorate in literature from the National University of Ireland on the strength of his writings. Perhaps, too, a long-standing concentration on fundamentally political questions bearing upon cultural and social issues leads eventually to a wish to explore other fields and other levels of communication in such a mind as we find in Dr Fennell.

While one may – indeed, must – refer admiringly to the crystalline clarity of so much that Desmond Fennell has written, it is not to be supposed that his immersion in certain areas of human experience can be uncomplicated or is, I think, evenly balanced.

The journal *InCognito* in 1999 published his essay 'Three Views of Reality: The Poetry of Higgins, Kavanagh and Heaney'. In that he has written:

> It is common knowledge that the Irish literary renaissance included efforts by Irish writers to depict 'the real Ireland', as distinct from 'unreal', inauthentic or superficial Ireland. But the most serious participants in this project, like all serious literary artists, were also, and fundamentally, concerned with representing reality in general: *reality as such....*
>
> Kavanagh's attack on the Higgins kind of poetry contained an implicit statement of his own view of the real and of how it must be represented. While excoriating intangibility, he spoke for transcendence of the merely visible.... Reality... is both very tangibly material and absolutely non-material, with the matter having its ground and completion in immaterial being. We have seen Kavanagh, from his stance in that conviction, rejecting Higgins' immaterialism....

In the Irish context, Higgins' view of the real is, of course, a late outreach of the Celtic Twilight mentality.... By 1947, not only Yeats, but most English Irish poetry had long moved beyond the Celtic Twilight (Gaelic Irish poetry was never touched by it).... As early as 1909, Synge had rejected the Twilight mode....

Kavanagh, then... aware that he might be understood as including in his rejection the leading poet of the Twilight, W. B. Yeats ... was careful to make clear that he could recognise a great poet transcending his own weaknesses. After remarking on how difficult it was for Irish Protestants to be good poets, he interrupts his diatribe to remark: 'Yeats got there by being himself, by being a sincere poet. He dug deep beneath the variegated surface to where the Spirit of Poetry is one with Truth. I say this with reservations, but none the less it is largely true.'

Higgins' worldview had a second Irish context. Kavanagh was on firm ground – intuitively, on firmer ground than he knew – when he attributed what he found repugnant in Higgins's poetry to his, and similar poets', Irish Protestantism. What he had principally in mind, and said, was that their Protestantism impelled them to falsity in their attempts to 'be Irish'.

Dr Fennell then went into a passage that I found a little bizarre but was drawn from Roy Foster identifying 'a Protestant predilection for the occult' in *Paddy & Mr Punch: connections in Irish and English history* (1993). Not that Fennell quite allows himself the luxury of supposing the Protestant tradition to be a wholesale flight into immaterialism. No, listen:

Kavanagh's 'matter transcendent' was orthodox Catholicism. More than that, it was orthodox

Christianity. It was the view of the visible world that had been reflected in most of the art, literature, philosophy and mysticism of Western Europe until the seventeenth century. Active, in that century, in Protestant minds, it inspired the greatest Dutch painting and English 'Metaphysical' poetry. ... By contrast, in English-speaking Catholic Ireland, this Christian or 'incarnational' materialism had rarely found notable expression in any form. Kavanagh's poetry is one of the few literary instances of it.

But Dr Fennell did take, without admitting what he was doing, exceptions from the general Protestant tradition. He is a little more elusive about Heaney – because, one is given to think, of Heaney's ambiguities, and we are perhaps encouraged to think that Heaney has been influenced by post-seventeenth-century Protestant literary immaterialism. But really Desmond would need to deal effectively with what is most substantial in Irish Protestantism at that point, whatever its all too many general mistakes and sins in the Irish religio-political scene.

There is little evidence of Desmond Fennell taking authentic, unsuperficial Protestantism seriously. You see what I mean by ideology? It is not difficult to accept R.H. Tawney's theory about Protestantism and capitalism in *Religion and the Rise of Capitalism* (1926), but the reader of history who cannot welcome and celebrate the vast contributions made by Protestantism to what Fennell would term, in an appreciative spirit, humanism – at best Christian humanism – would be very bound by ideology indeed. After having lectured in University College, Galway, 1976–1982, on Politics and Modern History, and on Communications in Dublin, 1982–1993, Dr Fennell now lives near Rome. Perhaps the Italians are less familiar with Protestant challenge (both negative and positive) than Irish people?

In his book *The Postwestern Condition: Between Chaos and Civilisation* (1999) Dr Fennell writes of an epochal breakdown of civilisation in the West since the mid-1940s. He raises questions worthy of close attention. But, as a person who believes in a united, collaborating world rather than a Europe or a West re-organising its potential more or less unilaterally, I find an implied stress on this in the book disappointing. And I would think references to 'the Christian Church' might very easily have more substantial meaning than Dr Fennell's to 'the Catholic Church', by which, clearly, he means the Roman Catholic Church.

In his postscript to *Mainly in Wonder* in February 1958 he declared himself – emotionally and intellectually, I think – a European (pp. 271–272):

> I do not know so many things about men, the world and God as I used to think I knew. But the few things I know, I know better. The East really taught me man ... The first imperative purpose of any society – of all its wisdom, morality and jurisprudence – must be to ensure that the children shall have rice or bread.
>
> This task requires the building of an edifice of trust.... Loyalty and truth ... are the primary virtues. An untrue word or act strikes at the basis of society and at the existence of each individual and is therefore the essential sin. ... Man must be permitted ... to love.
>
> ... Belief and love are not hungers only but necessary daily breads.
>
> Ravenous hunger for these breads has characterized the European peoples and that Western World – from Santa Fe to Moscow – to which Europe has given birth. For Europe brought more to the world than the science and technology which ensured material abundance (rice

or bread). Europe injected the whole earth with her own hungers for belief and love – and she gave doctrines for the beliefs to cling to, ethics which enabled love to expand. Thus did Europe in the twentieth century after Christ make the world One.

Now, I mistrust that sort of talk. It seems to me dangerous because almost certainly deluded. My fundamental confidence that every human society can make some significant contribution is based on the Christian notion of universal love, but that idea seems menaced by what I read into such a declaration as Desmond made upon returning to Ireland at that time, and which I still find echoes of in what I think is his latest available book, *The Postwestern Condition*. Those words of his have a very important degree of truth, but also, I think, a European vanity that pays too little attention to the great achievements of non-Europeans. It is all too easy to fall for puerile generalisations – the dynamic West and so on. When modern Europeans confer with non-Europeans, they should be in a learning mood as well as a sharing mood in which one rather humbly advances certain things that we Europeans think were good in our experience – with a proper modesty, knowing how appallingly we have betrayed others. Because Europeans, for all their fine talk, have much too often not shown love. Every people can reach out for love – and, thankfully, not just reach out to Europe, but to God.

MAKING ARGUMENT WORK:
THE CASE OF FEMINISM

MARY CULLEN

DESMOND FENNELL stands out as somebody consistently willing to express his opinion publicly on a wide range of issues, and to disagree with what he perceives as the generally accepted or fashionable point of view. For this willingness, something relatively rare in Ireland and maintained over many years, I admire and respect him. This was one good reason to accept the invitation to contribute to this book. Another was the conviction that in Ireland we need to answer, respond to and engage with each other's ideas and develop ongoing debate and dialogue. Some years ago Desmond told me how frustrating he found it to publish a book or article in which he challenged accepted views and to get no response, no engagement, no argument. I know that others have suffered similar frustration. It seemed that not to contribute would be a failure of commitment on two fronts.

However, while admiring and respecting what he did, more often than not I found myself in disagreement with much of what he said. This presented a problem. Eventually it appeared that the best tribute I could make would be to respond to some of his comments on feminism and to try to do this in the kind of exploration of ideas I think we need and Desmond wants. This was motivated partly by the belief that if we are to develop public discussion in Ireland we need to manage dissent and argument more constructively than at present, and partly by the conviction that the potential of feminist thinking is seriously underdeveloped in Ireland and that this is a loss to us all.

We need dissent and we need both debate and dialogue. As was pointed out to me recently, the latter two are not the same thing. Debate, according to Collins' dictionary (millennium edition, 1998), is 'formal discussion ... in which opposing arguments are put forward' or 'the formal presentation and opposition of a specific motion...'. Dialogue is 'conversation between two or more people', or 'an exchange of opinions on a particular subject.' We need dissent and disagreement, and lots of both, but for these to be productive, for us to derive benefit from the clash of different views, they need to be expressed within the context of both debate and dialogue.

A good deal of public discussion in Ireland is conducted as neither debate nor dialogue. Time constraints on radio and television discussion encourage over-simplified expression of positions and make it difficult to evaluate and give credit to opposing arguments. They encourage presenters to sum up at a simplified level and to push the discussion in an adversarial direction as 'good' radio or television. Not many newspaper columnists engage in debate and dialogue in the sense of exploring different approaches to the subject in question and evaluating them. A few adopt surprisingly adversarial stances and combative language that seem aimed more at attacking perceived opponents than in trying to present an unbiassed summary of the disputed position and then advancing counter-arguments.

When argument is based on a belief in mutually exclusive positions, one of which must be right and the other wrong, it not only avoids serious consideration of important issues, but actively inhibits it. The recent public debate about the Nice Treaty provided many examples of this, including the letter written by one politician to the *Irish Times* in which he simply listed the names of six opponents of the Treaty as his argument in favour of it.

The adversarial method is not the only model for disagreement, and as a method of discourse it lessens the possibility of gaining new insights, or of finding the possible flaws and gaps in our own thinking that a different form of discussion might reveal. It encourages a degree of intellectual laziness in that it does not challenge participants to try to see what is valid in opponents' arguments as well as what is invalid. It does not facilitate engagement with new ideas, or learning from them, or looking for points of agreement as well as on disagreement. Some weak links in a chain of argument do not necessarily make a whole point of view invalid or fruitless.

For whatever reasons, few of us in Ireland show much confidence in our ability to engage freely with new or opposing ideas, and we seem to feel threatened by the possibility of having to change or even modify our opinions. We appear to have low levels of intellectual curiosity or of delight in teasing out ideas, testing their strengths and weaknesses, entertaining and exploring new points of view, moving on and developing our thinking.

We have few forums where sustained debate and argument about ideas are joined in by a wide range of people, and it is noticable that academics seldom engage actively in ongoing public discussion. We have far too little sustained debate and dialogue about issues of fundamental public importance such as the current form of global capitalism and the general unquestioning acceptance of it by the Irish establishment, and no serious analysis of the value system and implicit view of human nature that underlies it.

For debate and dialogue to have a real chance of influencing the value systems and thinking of society we need forums where as many perspectives as possible are assured of being listened and responded to, though not necessarily of winning assent; where argument and disagreement are not seen simply as battles between sectional interests but as part of a process that hopes to develop a form of consensus which could actually contribute to public policies which genuinely tried to further the interests of all the people.

Feminism, in my view, has a lot to offer to this kind of debate and dialogue and also has a lot to lose by its absence. I think it is accurate to say that Desmond Fennell's attitude to feminism is generally critical, but some of his criticism touches on important questions. Here I want to take his comments on two aspects of feminist thinking, gender and equality, published in a recent book, and consider how serious debate and dialogue about each could contribute to debate about the kind of society most of us would like to develop.

The first issue is the concept of gender about which he writes:

> There is a fine theological point which I would need to clarify by talking to some high feminists. I have treated women as one of the 'different' categories that are to be respected by the white-male norm because multi-culturalism, in its extended version, often does this *e.g.* in the common conjunction 'minorities and women'. At the same time, the very influential feminists who depict gender as 'construction' seem to be denying the *différence* that most men have traditionally celebrated, and saying that men and women are essentially the same![1]

First it is important to point out that, contrary to Desmond
Fennell's impression, there is no higher feminist authority
which rules on orthodoxy and heresy. Feminist theory is, as the
volume of publication attests, a vigorously disputed arena.
Regarding gender, Fennell is correct when he understands it as
construction, though not in thinking it necessarily argues that
men and women are essentially the same. It addresses the
distinction feminists make between biologically-determined
behaviour on the one hand and societies' prescriptions as to the
proper or acceptable behaviour of males and females on the
other hand. The latter is what is meant by the social
construction of sex and the word gender was brought into use
by feminist theorists in recent decades to give it a name. While
some differences in the behaviour and thinking of men and
women may indeed be determined by biology, exactly what
these are remains to be established beyond dispute. Feminists
argue that many observed differences are the result of societies'
intervention. These latter can be evaluated and changed if
found wanting. Also we can and should critically examine
claims that biology is destiny and all human action biologically
determined.

The reality of the social construction of sex has long been
recognised and challenged by feminists. One of the best-known
pioneers was the English writer and intellectual Mary
Wollstonecraft, who published *A Vindication of the Rights of
Woman* in 1792 to dissent from Jean-Jacques Rousseau's views
on the education of women. In the thinking of the eighteenth-
century European Enlightenment and civic republicanism the
model of the good human being was one who used reason to
make informed judgments and to attain virtue. In *Émile* (1762)
Rousseau outlined his vision of the education that would help
the young boy to grow up to become an autonomous and
responsible citizen who made rational and virtuous decisions.

However, Rousseau also argued that girls should be educated on the opposite principle to boys, specifically *not* to become autonomous and responsible but to obey men. This was because women's role in life was to serve men's needs. 'The man should be strong and active; the woman should be weak and passive.' She 'will always be in subjection to a man, or to men's judgment, and she will never be free to set her opinion above his own.'[2]

Wollstonecraft vigorously dissented and argued that women were rational human beings as men were and as such should be educated to become self-determining adults who took responsibility for their own lives. 'In fact, it is a farce to call any being virtuous whose virtues do not result from the exercise of its own reason. That was Rousseau's opinion respecting men; I extend it to women.'[3]

Around the middle of the nineteenth century in Ireland, as in other countries, organised groups of women, mostly middle-class and often with the participation of men, began to campaign to change the law on a range of issues. Their driving force was the fact that the legal and social restrictions imposed on women made it impossible for them to exercise control over the direction of their own lives, or choose how to develop their intellectual, political or cultural potential, or participate in society as citizens. Law, regulation and custom gave men control over women's lives. In Ireland, under English common law, a woman's separate legal identity disappeared on marriage and merged into that of her husband; he was the guardian of their children; he had full legal right to control, use and dispose of her inherited and earned property, with the exception that he could not alienate landed property. Women were excluded from the universities and the higher professions. The only occupations open to middle-class women who had to earn their own living were of low status and low pay, such as governessing and needle-work. Women were barred from political participation as government ministers, as members of elected representative bodies and from voting in elections. Double standards in sexual matters operated so that in what the law saw as sex-related crime, adultery, prostitution and illegitimate births, women were the guilty and punishable party.

In the campaigns to change the law in these areas women's emancipationists were campaigning for equality with men. This was the only model of freedom and participation to hand. But equal rights were not an end in themselves; they were seen as the prerequisite for full personhood and the gateway to active citizenship. From Wollstonecraft's demand that women as well as men be educated to be 'rational creatures and free citizens' to the 1912 motto of the feminist newspaper, *The Irish Citizen*, 'For men and women equally the rights of citizenship; from men and women equally the duties of citizenship', the feminist demand was for the rights that would give them control over their own lives and allow them to shoulder their share of responsibility for how society was organised and managed.

The feminist campaigns eventually succeeded in removing most of the overt discriminations. In Ireland the 1922 constitution of the Free State gave full equality of citizenship to both sexes. At this stage women in Ireland, like women in other countries, discovered that the removal of legal barriers was not enough to change the model of female subordination in both male and female minds and that in practice many barriers remained. This was recognised by the second wave of feminism which reached Ireland from America in 1970 with the Women's Liberation Movement. Its main focus was on raising women's awareness of the power that gender models of masculine authority and leadership and female subordination and passivity still exercised over both sexes. It hoped that this awareness would then unleash a mass wave of confidence and energy that would sweep away remaining discriminations and allow women to achieve their full potential.

The historical context helps us to see the significance of the concept of gender. It allows us to compare and analyse the ways in which women have found that the stereotype or model of femaleness presented to them by their society did not correspond to their knowledge of their own capabilities and ambitions and that it was a less-than-human model. Typically these stereotypes omitted the essential human attributes of autonomy and responsibility for one's own life. Gender analysis allows us to see, name and put into words this reality. Until an idea is put into words we cannot communicate it to others or even think about it seriously for ourselves.

The concept of gender can then be applied to different societies and different periods in history, acknowledging difference and change over time and place, avoiding the reductionism that would see all women as being oppressed by all men at all times in all places, recognising that women as well as men can be and have been oppressors, but insisting that the stereotypes of femaleness – and maleness – current in any society at any given time should always be open to critical scrutiny and challenge.

In this regard feminism faces a problem in that the use of the word gender to mean the social construction of sex has virtually disappeared in popular usage. Today it is in general use as a synonym for sex, as in 'we need a better gender balance in government, in the Dáil, in the judiciary, in big business, or whatever...'. It does not matter so much what word we use, but it does matter that the concept of the social construction of sex does not get lost. Awareness of the reality of this social construction was the original driving force behind feminism, and we need both to hold on to this awareness ourselves and to communicate it to others.

This links gender with the other feminist issue Desmond
Fennell refers to, equality. In *Uncertain Dawn* he argues that the
aim of equality and equality legislation are meaningless unless
aimed at equality with someone, 'equal to whom', and argues
that the condition of the 'normal white male' is made the
standard to aim for by feminists, multiculturalists and gay
activists.[4]

Fennell has a cogent point here and he identifies a
problematic area for feminist thinking. It must be conceded
that in most public discussion in Ireland it is taken for granted
that equality with men is the essential feminist objective, and
this is not publicly contested in a sustained way by feminists.
Most commentators appear to assess the level of feminist
success by a headcount of the relative numbers of men and
women in what are seen as powerful, influential or desirable
positions: government ministers, Dáil deputies, business
executives, judges, barristers, and so on.

Equality as a means to achieve authenticity as a human
person opens up challenges and vistas where equality as an end
in itself does not. I want to consider some of the thinking that
follows from awareness of the origin of the concept of gender
as social construction and of demands for equal rights and how
this might feed into public discussion of how we want Irish
society to develop.

The historical context briefly outlined above is something
that has not yet found its way into many survey histories of
Irish society. As the historian Arthur Marwick has pointed out,
what individual memory does for the self-knowledge of
individual men and women, the historians do for groups,
communities, societies and nations. What their books do not
include is not there in our memory. Most history has been
written from a perspective that sees men as the active agents in
human history and women as passengers confined to a

domestic role, which is not seen as part of the patterns of change and continuity for which historians look. So for women their past has generally appeared a blank. The gradual emancipation of women and their attainment of personal autonomy and equal citizenship appears to have just spontaneously happened. In reality it was achieved by long and sustained campaigns to change laws, regulations and customs, often against vigorous opposition. Even then unfinished business still remains. Not only has the memory of these campaigns themselves and what they tell us of feminist awareness been lost, but so has the memory of their underlying cause, the relative positions of men and women in terms of access to personal autonomy, control of resources, education, politics and more, in sum the gender relationships. These unrecorded historical realities also have obvious implications for men's group memory and the attitude of both sexes to masculine stereotypes. Indeed, the very fact that so much has gone unrecorded and the reasons for this are themselves a significant aspect of our history.

Women's emancipationists in the nineteenth century based their claims on two strands of argument. One was the Enlightenment emphasis on the equality of all persons on the basis of shared rational human nature. The other was that women and men made different contributions to society, that these were equally important and that women needed full citizenship to make theirs effectively. What was seen as women's work in the 'private sphere', care and management of the home, children and family, love and nurturing of individuals, was as important a contribution to society as men's work in the 'public sphere', and these values and skills were needed in both spheres. Liberalism had a lot to offer nineteenth-century feminists in its insistence on equality in the sense of the removal of all external barriers to individual self-determination. Feminists could and did argue that within their own terms of reference liberals must support the removal of all barriers based on sex. However, socialist feminists in Europe, notably in Germany, argued that equality with men within the existing political, social and economic structures would only benefit bourgeois women and that feminism should ally itself with socialism to achieve full liberation for all women and all men.

Today most public discussion of equality issues is conducted without reference to the historical context or to the blindness of historians to the political, social and economic consequences of being born male or female at a particular time and place in history. If historians of women can get their findings into what we often call mainstream history it would place today's discussion of equality between the sexes on a firmer starting ground.

Patriarchal societies have tended to divide human characteristics into 'complementary' sex-specific categories very much along the lines of Rousseau's 'strong and active' men and 'weak and passive' women. One range, including independence, leadership, ambition, aggression, assertion and self-sufficiency, is assigned to males, and another, including compassion, caring, dependence, nurture, gentleness, passivity and sensitivity to the feelings of others, to females. These are then seen as 'masculine' or 'feminine' characteristics, either as innate or socially desirable or both. Societies have usually tended to value the masculine attributes more highly than the feminine, as the concentration of so much written history on war and politics demonstrates.

There are several points to note here. Firstly, if the models are indeed complementary, it does not make sense to see either one as the human norm. Secondly, it can be argued that each stereotype contains characteristics that no human person should be encouraged to develop, such as aggression and dominance, or passivity and dependence. Each also contains characteristics we might think all human persons should be encouraged to develop, such as independence, assertion, caring, compassion, nurture. By feminist definition a male model that includes dominance over other human persons, women or other men, can neither be an acceptable human one nor can it be seen as the norm or the standard at which to aim. Feminist analysis suggests that we need new models for both women and men that will encourage love, care and respect for others along with love, care and respect for oneself. If authenticity as a human person is incompatible with subordination then feminism can only logically aim at the abolition of subordination for all women and all men, and at an organisation of society that allows every individual the right to self-determination in their own lives.

However, feminist awareness does not bring with it a blueprint either for the ideal human being or for the ideal organisation of society which would further feminist objectives. Feminists look for the way forward in interaction with other analyses of society coming from other starting points. The political perspectives most relevant to today's debates are liberalism and socialism.

Political thought develops in concrete historical situations as human minds grapple with the questions arising from contemporary political, social and economic circumstances. It develops and changes in interaction with changes in these circumstances, both contributing to and being influenced by them. Modern liberalism emerged as a middle-class claim for freedom from feudal and monarchical controls. It drew on the Enlightenment support for the equality and liberty of the individual and, in response to the industrial revolution in Britain, it linked with the interests of the new commercial, industrial and entrepreneurial classes to support the new idea of economics as a science governed by the 'laws' of the market. It produced nineteenth-century *laissez-faire* politics. *Laissez-faire* liberalism later accepted limited government intervention via welfare provisions. Today, in interaction with the current stage of globalisation of capitalism, neo-liberalism supports the argument that the uncontrolled self-interest of individuals is the best way to increase overall wealth which will in time increase the wealth, and hence the happiness, of everyone.

Modern developments in socialism grew from opposition to liberalism. Socialists also believe in liberty and equality but reject the capitalist separation of labour from the worker and his or her social context. Socialism takes many forms but essentially believes that society must in some way control the means of production in the interests of the common good rather than letting them be controlled in the interest of profits.

Today in Ireland, and in much of the developed world, the liberalism versus socialism argument appears over for many people with the basic question whether the state or the market have primary control over economic development and economic activity decisively settled in favour of the latter. In Ireland the consensus among most political parties and commentators seems to accept the values of the current state of development of global capitalism as the norm and also as desirable. Individual freedom and equal rights and equal opportunity are accepted as being the right to compete in a system where it is in the best interests of the common good that competition for profit is the dominating objective. This should be as unrestricted by government control as possible. It will then produce the maximum wealth for the winning interests and individuals and this will in turn benefit everybody by a trickle down effect. The unspoken premise is that increased wealth for individuals is sufficient by itself for increased happiness.

So feminism would first ask how far feminist objectives can be realised in terms of today's unregulated global capitalism and the liberal theory of individual freedom underpinning it? Feminists have campaigned so that women would have the right to work outside as well as inside the home. Has today's uncontrolled property market used that hard-won freedom to push up house prices so that couples are forced to both work in full-time jobs outside the home? Has the provision of child-care been geared more to the demands of the market than to the real interests of human beings, women, men and children? Does the general acceptance that market forces 'compel' multinational companies to move production from one part of the world to another as profits 'dictate' with no responsibility for disruption to the fabric of peoples' lives, those of employees, employees' families and local communities, further or hinder feminist objectives? Does seeing individuals as economic units divorced from their social context foster autonomy, self-determination, or the possibility of new models of human nature and its needs?

What about socialism? As already noted, both liberalism and socialism aim at liberty and equality. In practice some of the twentieth-century experiments in socialism fell so far short of providing for individual autonomy and self-determination that socialism fell under a cloud from which it is now re-emerging as it becomes clearer that global capitalism may not be the panacea it was proclaimed to be. For feminism the basic question would be whether control of the means of production in the interests of the community instead of profits would better further feminist objectives? How could such control be achieved? Can the state be trusted to achieve it? What form of state? Ireland is a representative parliamentary democracy like most of the developed world. Currently most of these governments to a greater or lesser degree support the neo-liberal principles of the dictates of the market and the global capitalist economy. Do feminists need to join the search for more effective and participatory forms of democracy which might have a better prospect of delivering the basic democratic and civic republican ideal, government by the people and in the interests of the people? How can that be achieved if we accept that decision by simple headcounts and majorities will not necessarily provide conditions in which all women and all men can achieve full personhood? If there is no consensus on what comprises the common good then how do we accommodate that in a democratic way?

At present feminists in Ireland are not engaged in widespread debate and dialogue about such questions. In the 1970s and 1980s when feminism was something like a nation-wide community there was indeed political argument about feminist objectives and strategies, what these were or should be, and liberal feminists, Marxist feminists, radical feminists and socialist feminists vigorously contested the ground. But feminism has shared in the general decline of public debate in Ireland and the growing theoretical deficit

As a feminist who believes in the potential of feminist insights and analysis I would very much like to see a new feminist debate-cum-dialogue developing in Ireland. We also need serious feminist participation in public debate and dialogue about the future direction of Irish society. The feminist contribution to this would be vital. The logic of feminist origins and analysis does not lead to a battle of sectional interests between men and women. It points to the pursuit of an authentic humanity that can no more be claimed for women alone than for men alone. Feminist analysis demands that all women and all men have control over their lives, and share the responsibility for the organisation of society, and the creation of an environment that favours the development of more rounded human beings. It also insists that love, care and respect for other human beings cannot be assigned to a 'private' sphere of home and family, while a totally conflicting set of rules operates in the 'public' sphere. We all live in both spheres and what happens in one interacts with and influences what happens in the other. This realisation has been at the root of feminist awareness.

There are two sides to the argument being put forward here. Feminism can only develop its full potential and understand its limitations in debate and dialogue with other perspectives and analyses, while these other perspectives and analyses need the feminist contribution to develop their potential and address their limitations.

There are no easy answers and none of us has all the right answers. Real democracy in a civic republican context remains an ideal, but even if it is impossible to fully achieve it, the logic of feminist analysis suggests that trying to achieve it provides the most promising context in which to engage with and debate our various analyses of how best to organise society in the interests of the common good. The common good too is an ideal we will never fully achieve and there will always be disagreement as to what it actually comprises. Nevertheless it provides the most worthwhile objective around which to build constructive debate about democracy, a debate which can accept that mistakes can be made collectively as well as individually, that we can always try again, and which above all, in the context of what has been said here, tries to make real provision for ongoing dissent and argument.

I am grateful to the editor for the opportunity to respond to one aspect of Desmond Fennell's writing, and to Desmond himself for the challenge to try to articulate my own understanding of both feminism and constructive dissent. I will be surprised, perhaps even a little disappointed, if he does not take issue with at least some of my arguments. In any case, I have no doubt we will continue to agree on some things while disagreeing cheerfully on many more.

Notes

1   Desmond Fennell, *Uncertain Dawn: Hiroshima and the Beginning of Post-Western Civilisation* (Dublin: Sanas, 1996), p. 132.
2   J.J.Rousseau, *Émile* (London: Dent, 1974), pp. 322, 328, 333.
3   Mary Wollstonecraft, *A Vindication of the Rights of Woman* (London: Dent, 1982), p. 25.
4   *Uncertain Dawn*, p. 122.

WHY FENNELL IS NO. 2

BOB QUINN

DURING THE coffee break of an Aosdána meeting in Kilmainham in 1991, I found myself standing adjacent to the poet Seamus Heaney. For want of something profound to say, I inquired: 'How's that row between yourself and Fennell going?' He sharply retorted, 'How would I know; I'm only the subject', turned his back and walked away, leaving me with the realisation that I had become involved in a civil war of ideas.

The trouble was that my friend, Desmond Fennell, had been the sole member of the Irish literary community daring enough to publish a negative critique of his own friend Heaney's body of work. It was entitled *Whatever You Say, Say Nothing: Why Seamus Heaney Is No. 1*. My only personal interest in the pamphlet was that Fennell had dedicated it to me as a person 'who never says die'. Willy-nilly, I had been drafted as a foot soldier into the army of one general, Desmond Fennell.

Famous Seamus' snub did not bother me at all; I am accustomed to the prickliness of artists towards any criticism. I would feel the same myself. And the flattery of Fennell's dedication, whether it got me into trouble or not, was adequate recompense. But the incident forced me to do a crash course in

Heaney. Precisely because his poetry appeared to be extraordinarily popular, I had only glanced at it since his charming *Death of a Naturalist* made him the hero of southern nationalists in the mid-sixties. His prose, *The Government of the Tongue* for example, I found less opaque and Delphic than his TV utterances, and it was generously argued. His poetry I found pleasant and vaguely nineteenth-century-esque, reminding me of Emily Dickinson. It certainly had not the power of my idols, T.S. Eliot and Phillip Larkin, and was not obviously superior to the work of such as Patrick Kavanagh or John Montague. In a public reading that I attended, I found Heaney's persona modest and camera-friendly. I had nothing for or against the poet. I confess that I was surprised when he was awarded the Nobel Prize for literature, which honour I had thought was traditionally reserved for heavyweights. My own personal heavyweight, Phillip Larkin, had not acquired the distinction in his lifetime, so maybe it was all the luck of the draw, historical timing or, like many a literary award, a matter of fashion, taste, hustling, commerce and politics.

After the Nobel award, I read the second edition of Fennell's pamphlet, to which samples of verse were added. I found it equally well argued and at least politically convincing. Fennell's position was consistent. He had expressed a similar attitude in the early 80s in one of his *Sunday Press* columns. There he also uttered reservations about Heaney's poetry and had even joined the poet Seamus Deane as co-defendant to his, Fennell's, charge of their poetic timidity in the face of the Northern war. However, even I felt that this was already apparent; I had thought Heaney excused his position well in *Station Island* in a sentiment attributed to Joyce's ghost, which (*pace* Eng. Lits and my memory) went roughly as follows: 'You lose more than you redeem doing the decent thing; stay at a tangent.' There was a war on and Heaney's words were a sensible approximation of every sane soldier's motto in war: never volunteer for anything.

In fact, the only aspect that intrigued me in this dispute was that these three men were, or had been, friends. Fennell once told me that on their way in a car to a Field Day occasion in Derry, Heaney and he stood shoulder to shoulder in a *pissoir*. Fennell took the opportunity to ask Heaney what was the real pursuit of his work and Heaney replied: beauty. Which response made sense, at least to me.

The unusual thing for me, Southerner, was the public nature of the attack that Fennell had mounted on his friend. Such an action is usually unheard of in the South (meaning Dublin), where members of the literary community live in each others' ears. Private assassinations of public writers are the lingua franca of artistic conversations throughout the South. Prominent poets fumed privately at Heaney's elevation, but public silence was their order of the day. Unlike them, but like Heaney and Deane, Fennell's roots are in the plain-speaking, confrontational North from which he derives his forthright manner. Fennell spent a happy infancy and formative childhood in Belfast, until his parents came back from America and transplanted him to Dublin, a culture away from the grandparents who had hitherto reared him. For some reason the expression 'snatched untimely from that womb' comes to mind.

In Fennell's breaching of the Southern code I find a perfect example of why the man, while arousing ire, also demands respect; he is utterly fearless in the expression of his opinions. But in a culture whose essential characteristic is a facility for dissembling, Fennell's desperate approach has been a form of social and professional *felo de se*. And that, it seems to me, has always been his inescapable destiny.

Fennell and I are ships that have bumped in the night over the past forty years. In the sixties, I directed RTÉ programme discussions in which he articulately and bilingually (he is fluent in five languages) participated. He lived in Dundrum, Dublin, with his beautiful wife Mary, a biblical scholar in her own right, in a little gate lodge opposite the cemetery where two of my grandparents are buried. Our social circles – his, intellectual and artistic; mine, hedonist and alcoholic – rarely intersected, although he and the late Paddy Gallagher paid me the compliment of crashing my farewell party (I was leaving for Canada) in 1967. In 1969, when I had finally left RTÉ, Fennell chaired a meeting in Taibhdhearc na Gaillimhe. Never neutral or shy, he pointed out the flaws in Jack Dowling, Lelia Doolan's and my analysis of and, particularly, our remedies for, both national broadcasting and the nation in general. Having already dismissed the relevance of Dublin, he was disappointingly unsupportive of our campaign to reform RTÉ. However, it was the first time I heard him spelling out the 'view from the periphery' that had become so central to his vision.

If people have something to say and convincingly argue their personal perspective, I listen as carefully as I read – purely as part of the personal search for insights into the human and social dilemma. The popularity, political correctness or otherwise of ideas rarely bothers me. For instance, since Tehran, 1968, where I first purchased and read *The Thief's Journal*, I have been attracted to the work of the homosexual criminal and writer Jean Genet. Similarly to Francis Stuart, Brendan Behan and Pádraig Pearse, who each pilloried respectable society in their own ways. The idea of confronting society's assumptions, whether objectively right or wrong, and aligning oneself with the maligned, appears to me to be at least one valid approach to the absurdities and injustices of life. Admittedly, this approach may be a covert expression of psychological inadequacies, insecurities, buried hurts or whatever ills the mind is heir to – so be it; in case evidence is demanded for this sweeping assertion I can only plead the fifth amendment. It remains an intuition, supported by mere literature. Christ was crucified in the lost childhood of Judas.

Consequently, the consistency and defiance of the nay-sayers' approach, behaviour and especially the conviction with which they say 'nay!' is what touches and attracts the attention of a mental gadfly and agnostic like myself.

Thus, in Autumn 1970, when I was living on the dole with a wife and child in a Volkswagen van in Donegal, I wrote to Fennell. He had by then moved to Carna in the Conamara Gaeltacht and I had read about his plan to colonise this Irish-speaking area with thousands of *Gaeilgeoirí* – an ironic reversal of de Valera's 1930s scheme to colonise County Meath with Conamara people. In my letter I asked Fennell whether it was possible for such as I – a non-Gaeilgeoir – to also survive economically in Conamara and his reply was brief and confident: of course, it simply said. Come! Respecting his opinion – or clutching at a straw – I arrived there on a cold November night and knocked on his door. It was unlatched and unbolted. From inside a bedroom came the sleepy murmur of children saying that both their parents were attending the first Oireachtas na nGael in Rosmuc. We did not know where Rosmuc was located, so we camped for the night in the Fennell household.

Subsequently we lived in various rented houses in the area, including Rosmuc, and maintained a friendly discourse with the Fennell family. Thirty years later I still live in Conamara, like flotsam washed up by an unusual circumstance, happily above the high tide line. Fennell is long gone from here, but he left me with the above-mentioned 'view from the periphery', which has been fundamental to my work.

They lived in Muighinis, which seemed to be as far from Dublin as one could possibly move. It was an island, connected to the mainland village of Carna by a bridge of perilous aspect.

Very soon in his writings Fennell was referring to the place as Mao-inis to signify his approval, later withdrawn, for the Chinese communist cultural revolution. At the same time, Israel's revival of the Hebrew language was a matter of great import and admiration for him – it gave him the title 'Iosrael in Iarchonnacht'. This highlighted for me an apparent, but consistent, paradox in my friend's ideas. He was a staunch defender of Roman Catholicism as the necessary local and national expression of man's innate religious sense. I have no doubt that if he had been reared in China, he would have defended Buddhism. Therefore he took a practical and constructive interest in Church affairs, but at the same time preached radical ideas, which owed little to organised religion and less to international socialism. A friend of mine has recently called him, after a first meeting, a radical conservative.

In the 60s and 70s, possibly stimulated by the other revolution that was the Second Vatican Council, Fennell wanted the self-defined People of God to take an active part in the secular aspects of their religion. He was what the local people in Conamara called a stróinséir, a stranger or blow-in, and yet he had the temerity to go to the parish priest of Carna and suggest the formation of a parish council with teeth, one that would be more than a ladies committee charged with putting fresh flowers on the altar. Knowing Fennell, this may have sounded to the priest more like a demand than a request. However, the latter authorised his young curate to organise a poll among the parishioners as to the value of such an idea. The local Fianna Fáil hierarchy – the real hierarchy in those days – fought bitterly against this possible diminution of their stranglehold on all social affairs in the parish. Fennell was, not for the first or last time, demonised, but a courageous young curate was not deflected from his object and the parish voted for the desired council. It was one of Fennell's rare victories.

In his two-story, rented home in Maoinis I listened often and politely to this man's discourses on anthropology, geography, history and philosophy. His respect for, and knowledge of, classical Roman and Greek civilisation was impressive. Occasionally he would play popular songs from pre-war Germany and enthuse at the enjoyment of life they suggested. 'Celebration' was a constant theme of his, perhaps expressing a keen sense of its absence both locally and nationally. I myself was a fan of melancholy German lieder so there was a loose affinity of taste between us – even though Fennell occasionally trod a daring hairline between admiration for the historic achievements of the German nation and a clinical assessment of the nation-rebuilding techniques of the post-Weimar Nazis. If his ambition was the renewal of the spirit of an Irish nation – and I believe it was – then he was entitled to look for inspiration everywhere, be it Israel or Germany, China or Cuba. The scale of such a grandiose ambition invariably left me as a spectator, a *tiománaí ar an gclaí*.

On the importance of the Irish language and the Gaeltacht in the affairs of Ireland he showed no ambiguity. Being a Dublin gurrier I was then fairly non-committed to this dimension of national life. But Fennell's constant praise for the linguistic felicity as well as the ingenuity and energy of his neighbours was infectious. The irony was that at all times his Gaeltacht neighbours seemed to keep a wary, almost xenophobic, distance from his ideas for the 'improvement' of their lives. This was partly because they may not have received a clear idea of what he was really talking about but, more likely, because of his manner: an unconcealed impatience with what he perceived as slapdash thinking and an intolerance of a fatalistic or servile approach to life. It was very 'un-Irish'.

I must mention that, in mitigation for their less than enthusiastic reception of his ideas, the people of Conamara had

long been subjected to a procession of idealists coming from
Dublin to 'Save the West'. It was easy to fit Fennell into that
category in 1969. He was not providing summer colleges to fill
the B&Bs; he was not creating jobs of any kind; he had no
political pull. He was a mere writer. All he had was that debased
coinage: ideas. It didn't put food on the table.

Indeed, when thirty years later I directed a documentary on
the rise of the Gaeltacht Civil Rights Movement in which
Fennell played a seminal role – composing most of their first
list of demands – it was fascinating to discover that the same
wary attitude to him prevailed, especially among some who
might have mellowed into a sophisticated appreciation of his
motives.

Fennell's *Iosrael in Iarchonnacht* tactic was to challenge the
urban *Gaeilgeoirí* – whose revivalist ambitions he had correctly
identified as a failure – to come and settle in the place where
Irish was actually the first language. He suggested that the skills
they might bring with them – butchers, bakers, perhaps even
candlestick makers – were what Conamara needed to build
vibrant communities that might reinvigorate what he saw as a
depressed, dole-oriented community. The idealism of Fennell is
well illustrated in this ambition. The logic of his proposal was
impeccable and quite feasible if one was driven by the
desperation of, say, post-war jews, and facilitated by the self-
interest of imperial powers. He was aware of, but ignored, the
excuse that most urban Irish speakers are civil servants, locked
in safe pensionable jobs. To them, the idea of throwing up such
security for what they saw as the wilds of Conamara – from
which many of them had escaped in the first place – was a non-
starter. Fennell certainly roused the ire of his peer group,
successful *émigré* Gaeltacht journalists then prominent in RTÉ
– such as Breandán Ó h-Eithir and Proinnsias MacAonghusa. It
made for many acerbic public exchanges between them.

Fennell's nationalist vocabulary also became a soft target for the Workers Party members in that same organisation.

On the more important local front, he ignored the implication – which was perceived instantly by his neighbours – that historically they had proven themselves incapable of pulling themselves up by their own bootstraps. Indeed he had no hesitation in saying that they, like the general population of the country, still had 'the landlord in the skull'. This was not likely to make him popular either with his neighbours or with the urban *Gaeilgeoirí* who proclaimed their love of language, nation and Gaeltacht. Similarly, the idea of thousands of urban people with bad Irish settling on their poor but jealously-held land was not attractive to Conamara people either. In other words, and with hindsight, it may be said that Fennell's idealism confronted and challenged the fact that life in southern Ireland was and is approached as a matter of survival, a progress of small ambitions and negotiations. Without powerful political or financial backing, grandiose homegrown plans for both secular and spiritual salvation have no fruitful soil here. Even with such backing, many a grand plan has foundered in Ireland.

However, Fennell's ideas for Conamara were significantly endorsed when he and his young fellow-conspirator, Seosamh Ó Cuaig, travelled to a meeting of Conradh na Gaeilge in Dublin. Present was the living, patron saint of the Gaelic revival movement, Máirtín Ó Cadhain. This honest man stated publicly that he saw much sense in Fennell's ideas and, further, that he himself might have achieved more for the Irish language had he stayed at home in his Gaeltacht powerbase. After Fennell finally left Conamara twenty years ago, I made a documentary film in which he expressed his considered judgement on the place; the film was called *The Last Days of the Gaeltacht*. It won the premier award at the Celtic Film Festival of 1982. I have a vivid memory of meeting the writer in the

Skeffington hotel in Galway when it was clear that Conamara would no longer be his home. In response to my vague comment that he appeared to be leaving all he loved, he cryptically answered: 'too much sacrifice can make a stone of the heart.' I did not pursue the matter.

I appear to have dived in at the deep end in these comments on Fennell. Let me backpaddle to lighter matters. In fact, I realise immediately that such do not spring lightly to my mind. For Fennell, life appears to have been always real, earnest and short. His jokes and laughter have invariably resonated with irony and black humour. I do recall one of his children telling me how their father trained them not to stare at the sun and damage their eyes. He encouraged them to imagine that Mason Island, in the line of the setting sun through their front window, was a possible target for nuclear attack. Therefore they must shield their eyes from the sun as rehearsal for a nuclear attack. It was a grim, wildly unlikely, but effective preventive measure.

It illustrates a Fennell penchant for insisting on the relationship between immediate experience and the larger context, making parables out of apparent trivia, seeing a world in a grain of sand. This may be why he and Mary produced five intelligent, well-travelled and well-read children who, incidentally, do not lack a sense of humour. Long ago at my own dinner table I witnessed his daughter Sorcha, then a teenager, now an indefatigable Third-World worker, impressing her contemporaries with her charm and subtle awareness of world affairs. The psychic damage that all parents inadvertently inflict on their children does not appear, in the Fennell case, to be incommensurate with other people's experience, and certainly not with my own. But then, my lifelong motto is: knowledge enters through pain. It is no doubt a relic of the generation to which Fennell and I belong.

Which brings me to puritanism. Fennell once described a puritan as 'correct, self-contained, unsensual, pained by the world and himself, and disdainful of charm and communication because to be right is enough.' Many of his opponents would fasten on that as a crude description of the writer himself. As a friend I have to recognise the approximation, but regard it as quite inadequate to describe his complexity. Then, who knows anybody? Certainly the 'stating of truths' as he sees them, with conviction and passion, and an impatience with those who sit on the fence, is a prominent part of the Fennell make-up. One of his favourite quotations to me was from the Book of the Apocalypse, as I remember it: 'Because you are lukewarm; because you blow neither hot nor cold, I will spit you out of my mouth!'

That conjured up for me an army of *apparatchiks* scurrying fearfully around the thrones of their masters, practising the techniques of forced smiling, networking, speaking prudently in wisps and wraiths of meaning, keeping the lid on things, praising when it is superfluous, condemning when it is safe, exercising invisible sanctions, inhabitants of a grey Kafkaesque world. This bleak image must approximate to what Fennell felt when his career was sabotaged by the Cosgrave government in 1976. I have written of this elsewhere so, briefly, what happened was this:

He was invited by Dr Eoin McKiernan of the Irish American Cultural Institute to participate in a fourteen-city cultural tour of the United States. The IACI had impeccable credentials, was backed by the Irish Government and necessarily had to accept modulations of its tune as suggested by that Government. Thus when the Department of Foreign Affairs, at the instigation of its ambassador in Washington, objected to Fennell's participation in the tour, he was dropped by McKiernan. It was a cruel blow to an Irish writer who was circumscribed by the paper wall of the Dublin media, which itself was hamstrung by the British paper wall around Ireland. There were two additional ironies. Dr McKiernan replaced Fennell with yours truly, this writer, who was totally oblivious to the reason for Fennell's cancellation – until it was divulged to me in Washington at the very end of the tour. I realised that my friend had decided not to spoil my party. The second irony was that the minister for Foreign Affairs who took the advice of his minions and effected the guillotine was none other than Fennell's old schoolmate, Garret FitzGerald.

I assume this left a bitter taste in Fennell's mouth; but I am also certain that his subsequent lashing of FitzGerald in newspaper columns (the *Sunday Press* in particular) was not personal. It was based on the writer's contempt for, as he saw it, successive government policies of placating the loyalists and denigrating the nationalist population in Northern Ireland, i.e. what he saw as the Irish Government slavishly following a British line on the North for peace at any price. Indeed it has always been a revelation to me how Fennell can sit down with friend and foe and discuss their divergent views, forcibly yes, but rarely with rancour. I witnessed this phenomenon early one night in a near-empty Baggot Street club to which Fennell brought me. The first sight that greeted me was a handsome woman pirouetting alone on the dance floor. To my astonishment, Fennell, whom I had rarely seen attempting to tread the light fantastic, went straight up to her and asked her to dance with him – which she did. I studied the odd pair and admired the confidence and unselfconsciousness of this man who, as far as I could see, had two left feet.

The real insight was to come. An unlikely pair, capitalist senator Shane Ross and socialist TD Michael D. Higgins, were communing at a nearby table. Fennell, by general reputation an outspoken Catholic, defender of the Provos, attacker of the

political consensus and unashamed Irish nationalist, suggested
we join them. These three unlikely bedfellows subsequently
exchanged pleasantries for a while. I was the odd man out,
feeling exactly as James Plunkett once described, 'the gap in the
circle of my friends'. Outside once more, I asked Fennell to
explain the warmth between what I would have imagined were
deadly ideological enemies. 'Who else have as much in
common to talk about as political animals,' he responded.

I learned something about Irish political culture that night.

In preparing this essay I made two lists. The first consisted
of who and what Fennell has at one time or another publicly
and trenchantly criticised. It included Fianna Fáil, Fine Gael,
FitzGerald, Heaney, Hume, Tone and Davis, Trade Unions,
divorce, abortion, contraception, the Catholic clergy, Vatican
Two, the Church of Ireland, the modern Gaelic revivalists,
RTÉ, the *Irish Times*, the British Government, the Irish
Government, consumer liberalism, imperialism, conservatism,
sexual libertinism, the middle class, feminism, bureaucracy, the
colonising device of 'Celticism', incompetent local
government, the inertia of central government, Sinn Féin,
unionists, the United States and the USSR.

What emerges from this first list is a catholicity of targets.
Indeed, it contains a range of subjects that is the staple diet and
target of most working journalists. It does not support the image
of a narrowly conservative ideologue, as Fennell is frequently
portrayed by those who have never read his more complex
works. If anything, it suggests the broad range of interests of any
educated, middle-class person. What it might also illustrate is
that a speed-reading audience is less moved by the content of an
argument than by the body language and tone used to convey it.
Form transcends content. Fennell speaks as he writes: with
supporting clauses and many emphases, the latter usually
signalled by his frequent use of italics in case we should miss one

of his more subtle points. This may sometimes appear patronising and can certainly distract from his core arguments.

The second list I made was more difficult to fill in: for whom and for what does Fennell express affection or approval? I once asked the following question of Anne Harris, deputy editor of the *Sunday Independent* and admirer of Conor Cruise O'Brien: knowing as we all do what O'Brien despises, I asked, what does the man love? She smiled her beautiful smile and said: 'That is a very clever question.' A question she did not answer. What a person loves is more revealing than what they hate.

In relation to Fennell I racked my brains and came up with the following list of what he approves, or at least of what he at some stage approved: Francis Stuart, Charles Haughey, Camille Paglia, James Connolly, George Russell, Pádraig Pearse, the film *Odd Man Out*, the working class, Christianity, the creative members of the bourgeoisie, hence Edward Maguire's painting, Mary Kenny, Nuala O'Faolain, Brian Friel's *Translations*, Tom Murphy's *The Gigli Concert*, the Israelis, the Palestinians, the IRA, E. Schumacher's *Small is Beautiful*, his wife and children, Italian Art, German philosophy, Heidegger's humanism, Sister Stanislaus, Margaretta D'Arcy, celebration, Olivia O'Leary, local initiative and Tom Barrington.

Any attempt by me to analyse these lists, to systematise them, find a thread, make a clear unambiguous statement about Fennell would be fruitless. First of all, I am not equipped to find auguries in entrails; secondly, I approach each person as a welcome example of the diversity of our species and the greater the difference the less likely to succumb to the dreaded homogenisation. Let the lists speak for themselves. Let me confine myself to an area about which I am more qualified to give impressions: the realm of the senses.

In 1969 Seosamh Ó Cuaig and Fennell – who despite an age difference had in common their respective attempts to understand, explain and affect social and political reality as it impinged on Conamara – set out in Ó Cuaig's car on the previously-mentioned journey to meet Conradh na Gaeilge. It rained all the way and the windscreen wipers were faulty. The two men talked intently, as was their wont, all the way. Ó Cuaig occasionally remembered to hop out to rub a half-potato over the windscreen and thus achieve moderate visibility. When they arrived in Dublin, Fennell noted for the first time the deficiencies in the wiper aparratus and kindly brought the matter to Ó Cuaig's attention. Ó Cuaig patiently responded that it had been malfunctioning since they left Conamara. Why then, demanded Fennell with a puzzled air, did you not repair it before we left? This to a close friend and fellow intellectual who was equally undistinguished in things mechanical and who, when he brought the same car into a garage in Indreabháin, Conamara, accepted the proprietor's gloomy prognosis: 'Ah, a Josie, tá tú ag tempteáil Fate.'

Fennell reminds me of Socrates, who, pondering certain geometric problems in the sand before being taken away to be executed, uttered his only concern: do not disturb my circles.

On another occasion he borrowed my rubber boots to walk in the garden. Half-way round he stopped and declared that he would walk no further in such ill-fitting boots. Their removal revealed that he had not noticed my old socks were stuffed in the bottom of them. Fennell's tolerance of the discomfort reminded me of the Irish chieftain who did not flinch when St Patrick's sceptre impaled his foot, imagining that it was part of his baptism ceremony. This might suggest that Fennell is not truly immersed in the 'sensible' world, that his encounter with the scruffy reality of human existence is tangential, secondary to his attempts to make intelligible, to put in words and recommend remedies for, those aspects of existence that we prosaic mortals resignedly accept. All I have to say to that suspicion, even if it were justified, is that it would be a sad society that could not accomodate such a philosophic personality.

And accidentally I appear to have arrived at my main point: the apparent resentment of official Irish society toward the ideas of Fennell. This confuses me because I am aware that, before he abandoned Ireland in disgust for Italy nearly five years ago, Fennell was on friendly terms with many of the formative elements in Dublin society. My natural scepticism suggests the possibility that the very people whom he considered as friends were in fact *apparatchiks*, even carpet-baggers in the new social reality whose deficiencies he endlessly highlighted. For instance, one of his oldest friends was the mistress of one time Taoiseach Charles J. Haughey, with whom he was also on speaking terms. If he had access to such powerful people why did his ideas not impinge on their decisions? Or, at least, why did he never secure what they call 'advancement'. It seems sadly clear that his particular brand of social idealism was not, at that given point in our history, the one chosen pragmatically to sanctify present political and economic actions? I remember once chauffering Fennell out to Kinsealy, Dublin seat of Haughey, precise mission unknown, waiting patiently outside the gates and noticing the dissatisfaction of Fennell's demeanour when he finally emerged. I know that Fennell admired the independence of Haughey's stance on the Falklands War and that he expressed considerable disappointment at the man's subsequent stances when in power. On the occasion of this visit, I hardly think that he was asking the Taoiseach to invade the North, and in fact I did not inquire too closely about what had transpired at their meeting. The very fact that he could visit the Boss in his own home is what impressed me. I am easily impressed.

I have only recently begun to suspect why Fennell's ideas may sit so uncomfortably beside our thrusting new 'global' culture: he is a heretic. I understand the term to mean a person who adheres to fundamental beliefs, once held by all to be eternal truths, which are now considered superfluous, even irritating obstacles to progress. I think of the fields and hedgerows that support ecological diversity but which must now be bulldozed to make room for motorways. The idea of a Catholic, nationalist, united and self-reliant Ireland is no longer sustainable, and therefore has had to be hastily jettisoned. All suspected fellow-travellers of such ideas are unsound. It is heresy to oppose this enlightenment. Heretics are not innovators but custodians of ideas. They are essential social brakes, a bit like parents who try to prevent their children from making the same mistakes as themselves. And we know that all children at one stage or another consider their parents to be, however lovable, tyrannical fuddy-duddies. It is no coincidence that one of Fennell's extraordinary output of books, pamphlets, monographs and articles was entitled: *Heresy*.

One of the heresies that he and I share is that the 'periphery' is at least as important as the 'centre' – in a society, in a country, on a planet. Len Murray, Australian poet, put it well: only flat-earthers think that the planet has 'margins'. This viewpoint, which was the cornerstone of Fennell's existence in Conamara, I have happily embraced. It was the fuel that drove me for four years to produce my *Atlantean* trilogy of films in 1984 and which I am happy to be assured still has attractive resonances on this island. I will always remain indebted to Fennell for this insight.

This Ireland – as Conamara poet, playwright and humorist Johnny Cóil Mhaidhc once pointed out to me – may be a small island, but it's a big country. Therefore, members of the same class tend to know each other, at least by reputation. Some years ago I thought it might be possible for Aosdána, the Irish Parliament of Artists, of which I am a member, to expand its criteria of creativity from the confines of poetry, literary fiction, music and the visual arts to include creative and independent thinkers like Conor Cruise O'Brien and Desmond Fennell. As constituted, neither Edmund Burke nor Tom Paine would have been eligible to join. I was encouraged in this ambition by the successful nomination – on the grounds of his exquisite prose and cartography – of Tim Robinson to Aosdána, a nomination I enthusiastically supported as a member of the Toscaireacht (steering committe).

However, when I privately inquired of a cross section of 37 of the 150 members as to their attitude to a Fennell nomination, only 14 replied. One wrote a huge 'NO' on a postcard, another an equally emphatic 'YES'. Most of the responses were sympathetic and supportive, but many expressed doubt about Fennell's chances of being elected. I was aware that members of Aosdána cannot be intimately familiar with every other artist's work and mainly rely on the recommendation of members whose judgment they respect. I was also aware that a timely exposure in the media of any given nominee can be influential; despite their popular image, artists are keenly aware of and sensitive to what is going on around them. In other words, they are human, therefore a negative media image can also militate against a candidate. The artists who responded, although mainly positive towards the idea, were keenly aware of this dimension and therefore pessimistic. At almost precisely this time, an article appeared in *Magill* in which Fennell was quoted as having severely critical opinions about Aosdána, the very body that I was hoping to persuade to accept him. I despaired of him then; the man has no concept of the slithering, political necessities of making friends and influencing people. Yet, allied to a substantial body of creative thought, would this quality in a prospective member not be invaluable to a body such as Aosdána? Not wishing to embarass my friend, I decided not to proceed with the nomination – yet.

I can think of several possible reasons why my fellow-artists – many of whom are as agnostic as myself – shared my fears about his chances. Firstly, Fennell's insistence that a partial step on the way towards Ireland recovering a self-confident identity (as distinct from the trading post status that it enjoys at present) would be through an admission and retrieval of its personality as, *de facto,* a Catholic nation. In the recent thirty years of revisionism of all things 'Irish', this is not a popular political platform. I am ambivalent on this specific issue; I am of the generation of Irish people whose religion equally damaged and spurred them on. However, any form of social cohesion – social glue, I call it – including Roman Catholicism, would be preferable to the spiritual wasteland we now inhabit. Indeed, most of the recent radical statements about our society have come exclusively from CORI, the Conference of Religious in Ireland. On the other hand, I stoutly believe that the fact of rampant anti-intellectualism – which Fennell considers to have militated against his ideas, although he himself energetically attacks the ideas of fellow-intellectuals – can be at least partially traced to a period when the Catholic Church and its gombeen collaborators dominated intellectual discourse in this island. It is hard to revive a worthy version of a discredited intellectual climate. What would, in my opinion, be more worth reviving would be the culture of the dispersed and gradually silenced footsoldiers and footmen whom the Protestant Ascendancy shamelessly abandoned in the southern part of this island. Their quietude left a stultifying intellectual homogeneity in the public culture, only occasionally punctuated by figures such as Hubert Butler. To put it another way, the Irish anti-intellectualism that Fennell properly excoriates may have less to do with the withering of, for instance, hierarchical Irish Catholicism than with the diminution of Protestant free thinking. In this matter alone I tend I agree with, of all people, Eoghan Harris.

My impression simplifies – and possibly distorts – Fennell's perspective. My comments are solely intended to emphasise that he examines problems that many of us sidestep. For instance, his early and repeated suggestion of respect for all the pluralist traditions on this island, especially including the Northern British, and the possibility of federal arrangements – a community of communities, as he put it, to assuage the ongoing antagonisms – long anticipated the Good Friday agreement. He is never credited with this foresight.

There is one subject on which it is hard to disagree with him: the eggs that were necessarily broken when the American omelette called 'women's liberation' was adopted by the Irish middle class. He was once kind enough to give me credit for the perception that there was a neo-Victorian dimension to this phenomenon. For instance, the indignation shown towards males who regarded females with desire, i.e. treating them as 'sex objects', tried to deny the most fundamental biological instinct in both male and female. The objections made for evolutionary nonsense. The ideological attempt to discourage men and women from regarding each other lustily belonged in medieval times. The parallel – and successful – attempt to portray men as the sole initiators and perpetrators of domestic violence has recently been shown to be also grotesquely unbalanced. Violence is not the exclusive prerogative of either sex. Fennell has been saying this unfashionable thing for years – as have many of the sane women and men I know, but *sotto voce*. The ideological revolution, necessary though it was, called 'feminism', may be likened to the opening of Pandora's box, an event from which some unmanageable problems were rashly generated. This apparent liberation, like the consumer culture that facilitated it, is – as is the fate of all revolutions – beginning to be questioned by the common sense of men and women. Fortunately, when by the opening of Pandora's box many blessings took flight, one remained: hope.

And hope may be what has supported Fennell's intransigent posture for the past forty years. He likes to quote my all-time favourite film maker, Ingmar Bergman:

> You see, in Sweden we have everything, or rather, we live in the illusion of having everything. But in the midst of this wealth a great emptiness holds sway... In my films I describe this emptiness and everything that people think up in an attempt to fill it, and I believe that in doing this I am tackling the problem of the present time, its most important problem, that is, how to give a purely 'welfare' civilisation a spiritual and human content. At all events this is the problem that I personally am concerned with all the time. Don't ask me to talk of other things – I couldn't.

By contrast, Fennell as thinker is driven to incessantly discuss 'other things'. In recent years he has broadened his palate to an almost apocalyptic view, pronouncing judgement on what he refers to as postwestern civilisation and post-modern chaos. Because his thesis – crudely, that western, Christian civilisation ceased to be either civilised or Christian at the moment of Hiroshima – perilously undermines the very ground on which we strut, the very basis of our confidence; it is not welcome. We are almost in John the Baptist territory here. This was well illustrated on his last TV appearance in Ireland some years ago when he was invited to discuss his latest book on the subject: *Uncertain Dawn*. The normal custom was that writers were accorded, at least initially, a fairly courteous reception from their host, whatever about the audience. On this

Late Late Show a chosen panel of hand-picked and intellectually lightweight hecklers effectively shouted Fennell down, preventing the writer from calmly explaining the basis of his critique. One of them even had the bad manners to plug his own forthcoming book. Gay Byrne sat idly by. It was a shocking spectacle, not just to his friends but to any fairminded observer. I half-expected to see Salome grinning in the audience. Part of the tragedy was that Fennell's own son was the producer of the show. I understand that, in a scrupulous attempt to avoid charges of nepotism, he had left the organisation of this particular slot on the show entirely in the hands of, perhaps significantly, a female researcher. This necessary professional decision resulted in a travesty of broadcasting. I think the event may have been, for Fennell, the last straw. He now writes from a village outside Rome where his latest daring has produced an iconoclastic 'Revision of European History'. Whatever one's opinion of Fennell, he can never be accused of absorption in petty matters; his canvas is De Millean.

And at the back of it all, what? Certainly he still retains the sense of wonder glimpsed in the title of his first travel book, *Mainly in Wonder,* and continued years afterwards in the deceptively clear reportage of his *A Connacht Journey.* Sometimes I have detected a personal quality that falls somewhere between naivety and innocence; equipped with this, he seems to wander through a world populated by three-card tricksters.

In case I have given the impression of an impractical dreamer, out of touch with the earthy stuff of life as lived, let me leave you with the following image. The thin soil of my Conamara garden rests on granite, is very soggy and difficult to drain. This requires the cutting of tiny channels through the unyielding stone. The last time Fennell visited Conamara, he borrowed my chisel and lump hammer and exited the house.

For the next couple of hours he was to be glimpsed, squatting beside one of these narrow channels, patiently chipping away.

I think it is an appropriate image for his Sisyphean life, which, though the above may have the atmosphere of an obituary, he is still fortunately celebrating.

AN INTERVIEW
WITH DESMOND FENNELL*

CARRIE CROWLEY

BROADCAST ON *SNAPSHOTS*, RTÉ RADIO 1,
22 OCTOBER 2000

CC: *Desmond Fennell, to a lot of people you were a familiar voice, not just literally, but also through your writing, in the late sixties, the seventies and the eighties here in Ireland. I mentioned to somebody that I was interviewing you today, and they said, 'Desmond Fennell! Haven't heard from him in the longest time. Or, haven't heard about him in the longest time.' And there was some mystery as to where you had gone.*

DF: Mmm.

CC: *And today you can clarify that mystery because you are now living in Italy! By a lake!*

DF: That's right, by a big lake in a town of about twenty thousand people north west of Rome; about an hour by bus from Rome – let's say like Newbridge in relation to Dublin. And I have the best of both worlds there, because I'm living in this town by the beautiful lake, and have a quiet life, to do my writing and to think about the nature of the world and mankind. On the other hand, any time I want to go to the big

* Reproduced with kind permission of RTÉ Radio

city of Rome, I take the bus or the train and I'm there pretty quickly.

CC: *And what is it about Rome that you like?*

DF: Well, Ancient Rome principally. I've always been an Ancient Roman freak. Temples and forums and that sort of thing, you know? And I've got the opportunity now, not just to do a tourist run through the ancient site of Rome, but if I go in to the dentist, to check up on that broken pillar I saw in Saturn's temple the other day and to see was it what I thought it was. In other words, it's part of my life now, ancient Rome. But, I didn't actually, I must say, choose to live in Italy, or near Rome, consciously. I wanted to live on the Continent, outside Ireland, and I took a long train journey to several possible places where I had friends, you know, to get advice on prices, houses for renting or for sale. I went to Germany, Mannheim down to Munich, over to Vienna, down to Rome. Went out to this town, Anguillara, where I knew a countess, an Italian countess, and she told me of a flat that happened to be available at that time owned by a Russian woman. And I looked at it. And so I proceeded on my journey. In the other places I'd asked about prices and things like that but not actually seen an available property. So, back in Ireland, I said what am I going to do, and it was the only place I'd seen that was actually available. Instead of waiting for information to come from the questions I had asked in other places, I just took the easy way and said 'Yes!', telephone call, 'I'll take that flat, in Anguillara, Rome.'

CC: *I know you said in an article some time ago that you feel less of a freak, that you feel more normal there. You have also said that there is no living space in Ireland for thinkers. What is it that you think sets you apart, or makes you less than normal in Ireland, and in Irish society?*

DF: I suppose that from the beginning of my life I've been very interested in man, in the human condition, and the wider perspective of the western world in particular. After all, after College, I spent years living on the Continent, in Spain and Germany. I'd studied a year in Germany and later did some work there and I travelled in the Far East. So I came back to Ireland in the sixties and got caught up in the Irish thing, very deeply, because a great wave of patriotism surged through me and I became a believer in the Irish Revolution and the possibility of realising its liberating, humanising programme. And at the end, as my interest in Irish things tailed off in the late eighties, and I became interested in broader matters again, I found that I'd nobody to talk to in Ireland. Because these things aren't really discussed in Ireland. I found that if I did come out – well, I found that even with my new ideas on the Northern problem in the late sixties early seventies – you're usually met by either total silence, which is the classic Irish way to finish off new ideas, or by nasty *ad personam* attacks, you know. The main thing is you lack companionship, you lack others who say, 'That's awfully interesting, I've some ideas on that too.'

CC: *Well is it that you're looking for backup and you feel that your ideas are worthwhile and that others should appreciate them or are you also looking for debate? I mean, would debate satisfy that need?*

DF: I want feedback, above all. Feedback is the bread of my life, you know. I don't think I ever have the truth, so when I throw out new ideas, I know they're an approximation, an aiming at the truth. I'm wanting people to come back, feed back, and to correct me. Truth emerges out of a dialogue.

CC: *And give you their truth.*

DF: Exactly! Exactly! I mean take … it's a small thing, but I was just thinking of it the other day … when I did my pamphlet on Seamus Heaney – which was incidentally the longest piece of writing on Seamus Heaney that had up to then been done in the Republic, twenty thousand words – RTÉ brought me on a television programme and the whole aim of the thing, from the beginning, was to prove that I was wrong. It wasn't, 'Desmond Fennell, come in here and let's talk to you about these interesting thoughts you bring...'

CC: *And what were your thoughts on Heaney at the time?*

DF: Well, simply, it was my thesis that his reputation was overblown. That he was a good poet, but not a great poet. But the point is, what is criticism about? About having views, different views...

CC: *Mmmm.*

DF: That's all! So you see, I mean, I was expressing my view, and I would have liked when the RTÉ television programme brought me in there that they showed some interest, instead of having lined up all sorts of things to make me ridiculous and wrong. And this is a classic example of what happens in Ireland if you say something new; you'll be lined up by the media to be shot down!

CC: *Well, were they not doing what we were just talking about...*

DF: I mean that's only a small incident, Carrie...

CC: *But were they not just bringing in other people to open up the debate...*

DF: No...

CC: *... not necessarily to prove Desmond Fennell wrong?*

DF: Well that was the entire purpose. Nobody was in the least saying, 'Now what you've said there is interesting. However, with that or this I disagree...'. This is the way conversation starts, the way you and I are talking now. This is conversation; it's not annihilation. Right? So I was just brought in to be annihilated because I'd said something out of the way. But we're taking one tiny example out of a career...

CC: *Is there not a possibility...?*

DF: I don't ...

CC: *No, hang on a second!*

DF: I don't complain! You see, I don't complain! I mean, I'm the wrong sort. That is what you began by asking me, why am I a freak? I shouldn't be around here.

CC: *OK!*

DF: I'm interested in all these odd ideas, so I'd better be outside, where I don't have the irritation, or frustration, or sadness or loneliness that I was having here. And I'm in a country now where I'm not involved in its politics in any deep way, but I have round me a world of more respect for intellect and for ideas than I had in Ireland.

CC: *OK. Let's come back to all that later on. I do want to go back through your life as well because you have had quite an interesting life. We're going to take a piece of music. Let's have the piece that, to you, says Italy.*

DF: Oh, well. The piece that I would pick for that is the 'Chorus of the Hebrew Slaves' from Verdi's *Nabucco*. Now it's not called that by Italians, it's called '*Va, pensiero!*' And the reason I'm choosing it as representing my Italian period is something I discovered recently, during the European football championships, when it was noted in Italy with some shame that the Italian team didn't sing the words of their National Anthem. And I asked an Italian woman 'Why?' 'Well,' she said, 'you know, we're not taught them any longer at school, and anyway, it's very complicated words, you know, very old-fashioned language. Actually, we have a second National Anthem that is much more popular in Italy, because it came during our Risorgimento, our national revival in the nineteenth century, and Italians identified under Austrian domination with the condition of the Hebrew slaves, so we sang that song as a song – a longing – for freedom.' So it's actually Italian National Anthem number two.

Music

CC: *Desmond Fennell, your first choice of music there, a rousing chorus, which you describe as the Italian National Anthem...*

DF: Number two!

CC: *...number two! Uimhir a dó! Let's go back to the early days for Desmond Fennell, which were in Belfast, but not with your parents – you lived with an aunt and uncle for the first number of years.*

DF: I lived with grandparents and aunt and uncle. My grandfather from the Sperrin Mountains, an Irish speaker in his youth, the man of most influence in my life (*pauses, overcome*), my ancestor, you know. So anyway, my parents were working in America, so I was left with my grandparents and my uncle and aunt and there I passed what they all say are the most significant years of a child's life, until I was three and a half. And then my parents came back and took me to Dublin. So, I grew up in Dublin.

CC: *And what are your memories of those formative years in Belfast?*

DF: Nothing. I mean, nothing that I can identify. I mean, three and a half years. My memories of child ... of babyhood don't begin as early as that. I know that I took with me certain pronunciations which only later in life did I discover everybody here in the South isn't saying. It's only in the nineteen seventies that I discovered that you don't say 'fud'.

CC: *Oh, yeah.*

DF: ... you say 'foood'. But I was saying 'fud'. And also, when I've drunk a bit my northern accent does come through.

CC: *Yeah. And were they your paternal family or your maternal?*

DF: My maternal.

CC: *And did you, I mean, after you left them at three and a half to move in with your parents, which obviously was a change, you might not remember it that well...*

DF: Oh, I remember being brought to Howth first of all. My memories begin in Howth and then subsequently in East Wall in Dublin where we were living. My parents were poor at the time; they had lost practically everything in the American Depression. So they came back from America not well off and having to start from scratch again.

CC: *And the idea in going to America had obviously been to make money, to make the vast fortune. What had they worked at there?*

DF: Well my father had worked, he was a manager in something called the Bay State Fishing Company. I think he sold, he marketed fish. Anyway, they came back and baby-snatched me from Belfast. It was a funny situation, as you can imagine, with some impact on the rest of my life, that my parents in fact intruded and took me away, my biological parents. Because I was with my natural parents, my grandfather and grandmother. I mean the ones that I emotionally felt as parents ... I was able to walk and speak at that age. Obviously able to speak if I had those Belfast-isms, you know.

CC: *But how many siblings were there with you? Or were you alone?*

DF: I was alone. I was the first. So then my parents had another child, a daughter, in America. And they brought that girl back. So I, in the move to Dublin, wasn't any longer the sole source of interest in the house, I had a sister competing.

CC: *Yeah.*

DF: But I'm only saying that retrospectively, naturally. I didn't think in those deep terms, Freudian or whatever ... at that stage.

CC: *You didn't feel your throne was usurped in any way?*

DF: Well, I don't know, maybe I did...

CC: *Mmm*

DF: But anyway, that's the way I came to grow up in Dublin.

CC: *Yeah. And the family that you had left behind then, I mean did they ever talk about the leaving, about your actually leaving them and what they might have felt.*

DF: No, but they were my mother's family! We went there every Christmas!

CC: *But it's a lot different to daily contact, and actually living together.*

DF: Oh yes. Well, I mean, they lived there, they had their own lives, naturally, they were my grandfather and grandmother and my uncle and aunt so they formed a household that continued, with whom I had many contacts, especially every Christmas until I was eighteen. That's a big influence, given the importance of Christmas in a child's life, you know. So, we used to get on the train and go over the Boyne bridge to Belfast, reach Great Victoria Street Station, to a house on the Antrim Road which was bombed in the war, and then a house on the Upper Newtownards Road. So yeah, all that Belfast myth continued, a big part of my life. My grandmother, when the door would open she'd usually be sitting, as I remember her, on a couch and she'd open her arms and say, 'My great, big son!' But, son, not grandson. Interesting, you know. So, emotionally, as I said, my grandfather … I was very moved when I mentioned his name there … he remained … I had some correspondence with him when I started moving out into the world. When I was in the Far East my grandfather was writing me letters, you know. So he remained a great influence.

CC: *When you say he was an Irish speaker…*

DF: Yeah, in his youth.

CC: *As you grew up, did you speak Irish or English?*

DF: English. He was interesting for me because he enacted the, if you like, typical pattern of my people in modern times. He moved from a rural, Irish-speaking situation to an urban, English-speaking situation, where he was a second-class citizen, by definition, in Belfast being a Catholic. But my mother, and this is interesting actually, my mother … they had a shop in Belfast and my mother as a child remembers when the country relations would come up they'd go with my grandfather into the back room and sit, playing cards and drinking whiskey, and talking Irish. So in my mother's memory in Belfast city, people – Gaeltacht people – were talking Irish. But my grandfather, when I knew him, which was a good number of years later, he had mostly forgotten his Irish.

CC: *When did you get interested in Irish? Was that at school?*

DF: At school, yes.

CC: *Or was it post-school?*

DF: No, no, at school. I mean, I was good at Irish because I was good at languages. I had a very heavily language-orientated Leaving Cert. So Irish was just alongside French, German, Latin and Greek.

CC: *And I know you went on to do language and history, then, at College, which we'll talk about in a while. But let's take another piece of music, and I don't know if you'd like to take a piece which reminds you of Belfast, and those days, or if you want to pick something else.*

DF: Well, I haven't thought in advance of one that would remind me of Belfast. I mean the only piece of music that reminds me of Belfast is 'My Aunt Jane'.

> *(sings)*
> *My Aunt Jane, she called me in,*
> *She gave me tea out of her wee tin,*
> *Half a bap, sugar on the top,*
> *Three black lumps out of her wee shop.*

So, that's a childhood rhyme I took with me from Belfast. But maybe we could have, since it's September, the second of Richard Strauss's *Last Songs*.

Music

CC: *Desmond Fennell. Strauss's 'September'. Although it is now October, by the time our listeners are listening it will be October, but I don't think any one will complain as I'm sure they were all delighted* *to hear that piece of music anyway. Now, I said we would talk about your studying, and your languages and history, which you did here in Dublin, but then you also went to Bonn to do a Masters.*

DF: That was the beginning of my foreign travel. My parents hadn't encouraged it very much, because my parents kept me very much under their thumb and were afraid of all the evils of the world, and...

CC: *And was it the evil world that you specifically would fall into, or that any innocent Irish person abroad would fall into?*

DF: Any innocent Irish person, yeah, yeah.

CC: *OK*

DF: No I didn't show any particular evil tendencies, it was their general fearful view of the world, my dear father and mother. So it was only, therefore, when I was finished my BA that I, for the first time, went off living on my own abroad. Not only abroad, but living comfortably, because I wrote to Bonn University and told the Rector that I would like a scholarship. And by return of post he said, 'You have a scholarship, for a semester, in Bonn.' They have two semesters in the German university year. Then during that semester I, through a friend, got a further scholarship for the second semester from the German trade union movement, because they were interested in my workers' history theme, that was the theme of my MA thesis. So I got a larger one. After that I had very happy times in the German student fraternity that I joined. Which meant a lot of beer drinking and special days out with the ladies. The 'ladies', as they were called, very formal, old-world kind of thing, you know.

CC: *It sounds suddenly like little, kind of, boat trips down the river ...*

DF: Down the Rhine! You are absolutely right! We would collect the *Damen*, as they were called, the ladies, in their parental homes. And we would take them to the boat on the Rhine and we would go down the river and get off at a lovely little town where there would be a café with *Kuchen*, those luscious German cream cakes and lovely coffee and a dance floor. And we'd dance with the ladies there, and then we would take the ladies back on the boat, home. That was a 'ladies' day' you see. Most of the days were gentlemen days, of course, were drinking days, you know.

CC: *And was it very proper, in that way?*

DF: It was formal in a way I hadn't known from Ireland. I mean, I encountered what form means, what culture means, on the Continent in general, I mean, France, Germany ... much more formal societies than we were, because their cultural forms hadn't been broken by history as ours had been. So, in an ordinary middle-class, bourgeois way, proprieties were observed by these young gentlemen. Well, young gentlemen, but most of my companions had fought on the Russian front. That was there too. I'm talking of the fifties now, you know.

CC: *And did you fit in well?*

DF: Well, I was ... *Ich wurde gekeilt.* I was approached, I was recruited to the fraternity. So, I mean, they had decided. They only approached people whom they had observed, and they decided so-and-so would be suitable.

CC: *And did they ever tell you what it was in their observation that satisfied them? Like what was it about young Desmond Fennell that...*

DF: No. I don't know. Maybe the exotic thing of the foreigner. There probably weren't that many foreign students there at that time. When we'd go to the home of any of them, their mothers used spoil me with buns and things to take away. They'd cook these things; they'd give me packages, and treat me like a son. I was brought into the intimacy of German life through that, you know.

CC: *Which we probably haven't always been allowed see, because of, say, the historical reference, we always think of Nazi Germany, but we never think so much of the ordinary German.*

DF: Well, the propaganda, of course, maintained by British and American films every night on your TV, ensures that you will think of nothing else but Nazi Germany. It's amazing that, when I'm in Italy for instance, one of my favourite television programmes is *Inspector Derrick*, the German detective series, Inspector Derrick being the genius detective. It's, of course, dubbed into Italian. It has been sold to a hundred countries; it is one of the most successful detective series in the world. It's never done in English. He's a philosophical kind of detective; he now and again makes weighty pronouncements on human life and contemporary mores. But my point is, one hundred countries, it's been on for twenty years, and that Germany that is reflected there, that ordinary everyday Germany, like you see America in American films, is never allowed into English.

CC: *Mind you, we don't really take foreign work in, anyway. We rarely dub series from other countries. Like, is there far more cross-fertilisation, you know, amongst the other countries in Europe than to us here?*

DF: Well far more in Italy, and of course, you would see a greater variety of films too, dubbed into Italian, because the Italian dubbing industry is huge...

CC: *Huge.*

DF: ...and extremely good.

CC: *And is that because we are an island nation, or is it because we speak English and therefore we get all the stuff from America, there's no need to dub, we get stuff from England?*

DF: Well, London, I suppose, even more directly than America would decide what comes to Ireland, because, London filters America, doesn't it?

CC: *Well does it? I think a lot of them come from American distributors, straight to Ireland.*

DF: Well then, it's the decision of the Irish distributors. But leave out the poor English who are terribly isolated mentally from Europe in these ways. In Ireland we are most unfortunate that we don't have other countries around us. We are a small country. Well imagine a small country surrounded by five countries, all speaking different languages. How much more stimulating it is.

CC: *We've got completely off track, we started talking about Bonn and your Masters. I need to get to your marriage and Maoinis and all those things that are of interest, but let's take another piece of music.*

DF: Oh...

CC: *And then come back to Conamara, and to marriage, and to family life.*

DF: Well, you mentioned marriage and I suppose there's a piece of music associated with my early years with my wife. The love-duet from Wagner's *Tristan and Isolde*. Tristan is dying and she's singing to him, it's very passionate and it's also very erotic. We played it when we were making love, my wife and I.

Music

CC: *Desmond Fennell, before the break we heard the love-duet from Tristan and Isolde, which you said reminded you of your wife, Mary, who you met while she was a student.*

DF: That's true, yeah.

CC: *You had obviously graduated then at that stage, had you yourself? Were you working?*

DF: I was working in a bits-and-pieces way. Well, actually I was with Gaeltarra Éireann, believe it or not, in one of my incarnations. I was manager of their Sales Office, and I was also doing art criticism in Dublin. In fact, sometimes I used leave the sales office to cover exhibitions, you know, in the afternoon. I was covering art exhibitions for *Hibernia* and the *Evening Press*.

CC: *And for Gaeltarra, you were selling what? Handmade fabrics or knitwear?*

DF: Well Gaeltarra was selling those things. All I was doing was sitting at a desk at the head of an office where people were processing invoices, you know. And my job was to keep the processing ... the paper circulating. That's what a manager does, I discovered.

CC: *Well for somebody who ... obviously to whom the intellectual side of life appeals greatly, was that a disastrous job to be in, or ... ?*

DF: Well I wasn't always doing intellectual things, I mean, I was the first Sales Manager in Germany for Aer Lingus, for instance. I opened their first German office. In other words, I was the opener of their scene in Germany, at the end of the fifties. I found an office in Dusseldorf, I employed a secretary, I had a little Volkswagen in which I was supposed to go around visiting travel agents and encouraging them to come to Ireland. So I've done practical things, you know.

CC: *And obviously enjoyed them ...*

DF: Well I had to make money. I don't make money ... you never make money with intellectual things, you know. Much. Unless you get into the academic career. I wasn't in it, obviously. So I had to do things to make money. When I met Mary, that was the situation, and she was studying Oriental Languages, that's to say, Hebrew and Arabic, at Trinity College. So, when we married, she continued for a year to do that. When we had our first child, Oisín, I looked after him during that year. Well, most of the time, when she was at College. So, that was the situation. She finished her degree.

CC: *And at what stage then did you move to Conamara?*

DF: The immediate catalyst was that people wanted to widen the road we were living on, and it meant knocking down the cottage that we were living in, so one way or another we would have had to move. The broad catalyst was that we knew we would never be rich, but we knew we could afford the luxury of living in a beautiful place, so we said we would have that luxury.

So, we looked along the west coast of Ireland, a bit like me looking later on my train journey through Europe, we looked at Achill, we looked at Ceathrú Rua and finally we settled on Maoinis, near Cárna, Conamara, and there we moved. That was the immediate thinking. Later, of course, we understood, that it had not be an individual decision at all, but that we were part of the Zeitgeist, of the spirit of the times, at the end of the sixties when people were doing this all over the world, moving out from the capital cities to peripheral regions and to small ethnic cultures. So we were just part of a general thing. Funny, how these things happen and only later do you discover that you're part of a spirit of the times. In fact, a thing too that is interesting in view of what happened later, we went to the west resolute that we wouldn't become involved in any 'Save the West' issues, which we had read about, of course, as Dubliners, in the newspapers …

CC: *But you became totally immersed …*

DF: Totally involved …

CC: *Cearta Sibhialta!*

DF: *Cearta Sibhialta.* Yeah, and all that. I tell the story of that in my book, *Beyond Nationalism,* how the human environment gradually impinged on me, and did not permit me to be indifferent.

CC: *And, did that in some ways take you by surprise?*

DF: Yes.

CC: *Or did it sneak up on you?*

DF: Well, it sneaked up on me. It sneaked up, and the fact that it sneaked up took me by surprise.

CC: *Yeah.*

DF: Because, there was a resolution against it, you know.

CC: *And what was the whole ideology behind the* Cearta Sibhialta? *What precisely did you want for the West that it didn't have, as you saw it?*

DF: Well it wasn't the West, it wasn't the West … I mean … the *Cearta Sibhialta* wasn't interested in the West, it was interested in the Gaeltacht.

CC: *Oh right.*

DF: And my particular contribution was this thing, the idea was that Gaelgeoirí from all around the country, you may remember this, should move into the Gaeltacht, with their many skills, and help to create cities, towns there. In other words, make it a representative but Irish-speaking part of Ireland. Because you see it wasn't, it was a poor, neglected, peripheral part of Ireland. So, that was that side, which we called 'Iosrael Nua in Iarchonnacht' and later 'Iarchonnacht '85'. The other civil rights thing was more a movement, from inside, of the new elite of teachers and young factory managers, who wanted respect for the Gaeltacht. It had been patronised before that, by the language movement. It was a good place to go to get lots of the right spirit and learn the language. But we wanted road signs in Irish only, we wanted the Oireachtas, the primary Gaelic festival each year, moved from its ridiculous situation in Dublin to the Gaeltacht, we wanted a radio station in Irish, we wanted self-government, ultimately, for the Gaeltacht. We wanted, in other words, to be taken seriously. And I was calling on the Gaelgeoirí around the country to come and join in this to make it a new Israel. Like Jews from all around the world …

CC: *Yeah.*

DF: …came and revived Hebrew in Israel.

CC: *Some of those things have happened.*

DF: Yes.

CC: *But, if you look at it, the decentralisation hasn't really happened.*

DF: No.

CC: *Aside from, say, An Spidéal anois, where you have TG4 and you have, you know, a number of different projects on-going,* Foinse

*the Irish-language paper is out around the Carraroe area as well. So
you do have employment, you know, specifically through Irish. But
other than that, the whole decentralisation thing hasn't taken off,
has it?*

DF: We won lots of things, but you have named exactly what
didn't happen. We didn't get self-government, we didn't get
rialtas, 'féinriail' – self-government. We wanted a genuine
regional government, self-government, and we didn't get that.
And the survival of the Gaeltacht depended on that.

CC: *Well, how about, then, the interest in Irish itself outside the
Gaeltacht areas, because there does seem to be an increased interest in
learning the language, a lot more children are now going to
Gaelscoileanna, a lot more people feel at ease speaking Irish in public,
where at one stage it was almost deemed something that should be
kept for the back room and the card game, perhaps, with, you know,
the people from the Gaeltacht community.*

DF: I'm very glad to hear that, Carrie, you must tell me more
about it some time!

CC: *You mean you haven't recognised it or you don't think it's
happening?*

DF: No, I'm glad to hear it. It's another matter entirely, though,
than the Gaeltacht matter. A lot of people being interested in
Irish is a lot of people being interested in Irish. But I mean,
what we were …

CC: *So for you Irish is completely separate from Gaeltacht?*

DF: Well, I mean what the Gaeltacht is, is people speaking Irish
as the language of their daily lives. That's much more that
being interested in it, I think you'll agree.

CC: *And how about individual households, then, who choose to do it,
but do it in a city environment …*

DF: I welcome all that. I welcome people having any intelligent
interest, more than consumerism, in their lives. So, more power
to them if they are interested in Irish. But, I mean, it's a

different thing. When am I going to hear about Clondalkin or somewhere going Irish-speaking? I'm not. So ...

CC: *Mind you, there's a huge Irish-speaking community in Cluain Dealgáin!*

DF: Is there, yeah?

CC: *Yes! And the Oireachtas was held in Clondalkin a few years ago!*

DF: I picked the wrong place then, didn't I?! OK! (*laughs*)

CC: *Well! Maybe so. Anyway, lets take another piece of music! And it is a piece as Gaeilge. It's an amhrán I remember from my Gaeltacht days as well. We used to all sing it!*

DF: It was one of the hits of Conamara in the seventies. We produced our own hits as part of the general revival, cultural revival of the Gaeltacht. It's 'An Damhán Alla'.

CC: *It's a great oul' song!*

Music

CC: *'An Damhán Alla', Desmond Fennell, which brings me back as much as it brings you back, today, to my own Gaeltacht days. When you were in the Gaeltacht, just to go back briefly, were you with kindred spirits. I mean, if it hadn't been for the* Cearta Sibhialta *and all that you were doing in that way, would you have met on another level anyway, do you think?*

DF: Not really, no, because, my difficulty there in the long term you see, was the dream, the unrealistic dream. When we moved *en famille* to the Gaeltacht, I was going to spend the rest of my life there; we were going to spend the rest of our lives there. And in the end of course, we found out we were city people. We were townspeople, we wanted the noise of streets around us, you know. You may ask, why, after ten years or so did we move into Galway? That's the reason. Apart from the fact, of course, that I didn't have much more, really, than a good-neighbourly relationship with the people, nothing deep.

For simple work reasons. After all, one's work does determine one's human relationships to a great extent ...

CC: *To a certain extent. Yeah.*

DF: ...but ultimately, you see, we'd gone out there into an environment where if we didn't both get involved in some workaday way, we were thrown very much in on ourselves. Mary was teaching in the local school. But me?

CC: *Mmmm*

DF: So the answer to your question is that the involvement through the Gaeltacht revolution, through the civil rights movement and the *Iosrael Nua in Iarchonnacht*, was wonderful because it gave us a direct link with, not only the parish we were living in, but the entire ...

CC: *Community at large.*

DF: ... the entire South Conamara area, *Ó Chárna go Bhearna*. Yes, I mean, rushing from Rosmuc *don* Cheathrú Rua to Cnoc, Cois Fharraige and all that. There were things happening everywhere. It was a very exciting time. One of the most exciting times of my life.

CC: *You say when you went there you felt that you, plural, would be there for good ...*

DF: Yes ...

CC: *...for ever. Aside from moving away from Conamara, yourself and Mary also split up ...*

DF: Yes. Later ... after we came back to Galway.

CC: *Yeah.*

DF: Partly because I got employment in Dublin, and because I'd found it very hard – once I'd lost a column I had in the *Sunday Press* – to get employment in the West. I applied for forty jobs, I remember. I was teaching, somewhat, teaching part-time in UCG, but the president at the time didn't want me to get a permanent job, he disliked me. And so there was no prospect there. And I got this job in Dublin, in Rathmines, in what's now the Dublin Institute of Technology, as a lecturer. So, there had, of course, been a strain on our marriage through, as I said, that isolation and the strange environment that we had gone into in Conamara, and also through the impact of feminism in the seventies. So simply when I moved back to Dublin, Mary didn't want to come. So I made my future life in Dublin and she remained there.

CC: *You say the head of UCG didn't like you.*

DF: Yeah.

CC: *Does that happen you a lot, that you rub people up the wrong way, or that maybe, you just voice your opinions too loudly, or maybe you demand too much attention for your opinions?*

DF: Emmm ... I don't know. I mean, about people in general, I have dear friends all over Ireland. I have very few enemies. There may be a whole lot of people who, for the reasons I spoke to you about earlier, are disturbed or annoyed by these new ideas that Fennell keeps coming out with. 'Blah blah blah, can't he leave us alone!' kind of thing. OK, that's maybe the case. But, I mean, you take that Heaney thing earlier, there was a big public outcry, 'Put Fennell down! He's all wrong!' Privately, on the phone, by letter, support was pouring in. There you are, caught between the elite, the media elite, the public-opinion makers and the ordinary people. It was a very interesting example of it. And I've experienced that again and again. I mean when I had my column in the *Sunday Press*, well it was a great column to have, in the biggest selling Irish newspaper, thirty-five thousand a week in Britain apart from Ireland North and South. I'd go up to Belfast, people would – from my picture in the paper – salute me in the street in the Nationalist areas. That was living, that's being a communicator, that's being a writer. In any pub in Ireland I could be approached by some stranger who'd say, 'Like your stuff in the *Sunday Press*'. That way, I've always been in touch with people generally. It's the elite, in inverted commas, that I've had trouble with, because I find them conformist and they find me different. Now, conformists don't like the different, so there can be a clash there. It's not about liking, it's not about, you know what I mean, 'Nice fellow or not ...'

CC: *Personal animosity, yeah.*

DF: It's simply about uncomfort, or discomfort, when you are faced with the freethinker.

CC: *I know when you were lecturing in Rathmines, at one stage you used to say, 'Pray to God for an obsession. Once you have that, you've something to write about.'*

DF: Yeah, I used say that to my final-year journalist class.

CC: *Well, what would your – if you look back at it, I mean we've talked about Roman civilisation, language, modern history, writing, the Gaeltacht – what would your obsession be, your principal obsession, if you had to put one of them up there on the list?*

DF: Well, I've just actually finished writing a memoir book* with that as a central theme. Having to think back, I'd say certainly, certainly from the time I went to study in Germany at least, I'd say man. The human condition. To know man, and what makes human beings tick. That's why I travelled to the Far East when I was twenty-six, to see the other half of man, having seen Europe, to see Far Eastern man. And after I had got man straightened out, sort of thing, got fairly satisfied that I understood, more or less, what made him tick (him and her of course, but *him* in the impersonal sense of the being, man), then my obsession became that of Camus, the French writer. He said that it's sufficient accomplishment in a man's life to understand the age he lives in. So my obsession became the age I live in. In other words, this particular slice of man, the now situation of man in the West.

* *The Turning Point: My Sweden Year and After,* published by Sanas Press, November 2001.

CC: *And will there in turn be a third, and a fourth and a fifth obsession? Must you have something to obsess about? Is that what makes you tick, as opposed to the rest of us?*

DF: I don't know! But let me interject: I wish I wasn't so obsessed with these weighty things, because everybody tells me, and I agree, I should be writing stories, you know. I would like to write a great best-selling novel. But, you can only do that when you've got the basic problems solved. At least, I can.

CC: *And can you not just chuck the obsession to one side and say 'Stay there!'*

DF: I have people urging me continually to do that. I suppose my son Cilian led the list. But others too, saying, 'Stop it. You're good at telling stories. Tell stories. Play! You've been serious long enough.'

CC: *Yeah. Will it happen? Will that day come?*

DF: I don't know.

CC: *(Laughs) Your final choice of music, Desmond Fennell. Lest people think that you have regrets about anything in life, you're going to set that record straight as well.*

DF: Yes. Well, Edith Piaf said it all for me, *'Je ne regrette rien'*. I must say, I've been attracted by that song for a long time and tried to live according to its slogan, and I've succeeded, I think, on the whole. But there is one revision I would bring in, as I've grown older: I do not regret anything I have done, even mad or irrational, I would regret some omissions. That's another matter, you see. But, since I think the song is talking largely about regretting having done something, I stand by it: *Je ne regrette rien!*

Music

BIBLIOGRAPHY

BOOKS AND PAMPHLETS

The Northern Catholic
An *Irish Times* pamphlet, 1958

Mainly in Wonder
London: Hutchinson, 1959

Art for the Irish
Dublin: Mount Salus Press, 1961
(First published as articles in the *Irish Times*, August 1961, and
in the *Irish Independent*, March 1962)

*The British Problem: a radical analysis of the present British troubles
and of possible ways of ending them*
Dublin: Sceptick Press, 1963

The Changing Face of Catholic Ireland
Edited by Desmond Fennell, with a Foreword by Karl Rahner
London: Geoffrey Chapman, 1968

Iarchonnacht Began
Edited by Mícheál MacCraith
An Caisleán Nua, Gaillimh: Iarchonnachta 1985, 1969

A New Nationalism for the New Ireland
Monaghan: Comhairle Uladh, 1972

Take the Faroes for Example: the arguments for self-government in the provinces and the Gaeltacht
Baile Atha Cliath: Pobal Teoranta, 1972
(Pobal Pamphlets No. 5)

Build the Third Republic
Cárna, Iarchonnachta: Foilseacháin Mhaoinse, 1972
(Articles published in the Sunday Press in the years 1969–71)

Sketches of the New Ireland
Galway: Association for the Advancement of Self-Government, 1973

Towards a Greater Ulster (1969–72): a view of the last few years in northeast Ulster and in Ireland as a whole
Comharchumann Chois Fharraige, 1973

The State of the Nation: Ireland since the sixties
Dublin: Ward River Press
1983 (2nd edn, 1984)

Irish Catholics and Freedom since 1916: a humanist essay
Dublin: Dominican Publications, 1984
(A *Doctrine and Life* special)

Cuireadh chun na Tríú Réabhlóid: aiste dhaonnachtach
Baile Átha Cliath: Coiscéim, 1984

Beyond Nationalism: the struggle against provinciality in the modern world
Dublin: Ward River Press, 1985

Nice People and Rednecks: Ireland in the 1980s
Dublin: Gill and Macmillan, 1986

A Connacht Journey
Dublin: Gill and Macmillan, 1987

The Revision of Irish Nationalism
Dublin: Open Air, 1989

Bloomsway: a day in the life of Dublin
Dublin: Poolbeg Press, 1990

Whatever You Say, Say Nothing: why Seamus Heaney is No. 1
Dublin: ELO publications, April 1991
(Revised edn, June 1991; American edn, Little Rock, Arkansas:
Milestone Press, 1994)

Heresy: The Battle of Ideas in Modern Ireland
Belfast : Blackstaff Press, 1993

*Dreams of Oranges: an eyewitness account of the fall of communist
East Germany*
Dublin: Sanas, 1996

*Uncertain Dawn: Hiroshima and the beginning of post-western
civilisation*
Dublin: Sanas, 1996

The Postwestern Condition: between chaos and civilisation
London: Minerva, 1999

The Turning Point: My Sweden Year and After
Dublin: Sanas, 2001

Selected Articles and Essays

1958   'Journey to Lucknow', *Threshold* (Belfast), Autumn 1958

1961   'The Face of Moscow', fifteen-part series, *Irish Times*, Feb-March

1962   'Will Ireland Stay Christian?', *Doctrine and Life*, May
        'Swedish Journey', *The Capuchin Annual*
        'Goodbye to Summer', *The Spectator* (London) 9 February (reprinted in The Washington Post)

1964   'The Failure of the Irish Revolution – and Its Success', *The Capuchin Annual*

1965   'Cuireadh chun na Tríú Réabhlóide', *Comhar*, Nollaig (published in 1984 as a pamphlet)
        'Dublin Attitudes to Painting', *Arena* (Dublin), Spring

1966   'Irish Catholics and Freedom since 1916', *Doctrine and Life*, Jan/Feb
        'The Terrible Beauty That Never Was', *Doctrine and Life*, May
        'Ireland' in *The Catholic Church Today: Western Europe*, ed. M.A. Fitzsimons (Notre Dame, London: Notre Dame Press)

1970   'The Irish Language Movement: its achievements and its failure', *20th Century Studies* (University of Kent)

1971   'The Desire to Make a New Age', *Doctrine and Life*, Jan-April

1972   'Connacht Family Life in Context' in *Community in the Making*, ed. Michael MacGreil (Maynooth: Western Student Movement)

'Beatha agus Bás Pobail', *Pobal* (BÁC), Márta go hAibreán

'The Irish Cultural Prospect', *Social Studies*, December

1973   'To Have A Nation Once Again', *Atlantis*, April

1975   'Six Years' Work for Vision', *Doctrine and Life*, February

1976   'The Irish Samurai', *Planet* (Tregaron, Wales)

'Difficult Men to Say Yes To', *Aisling 1916-76* (Dublin: Sinn Féin)

1977   'Where the Irish Language Movement Went Wrong', *Planet* (Tregaron, Wales), Feb/March

'Aprés 80 ans: Bilan du Mouvement pour fair revivre l'Irlandais', *Ar Falz* (Brittany), No. 19

1978   'More than the Fleshpots: on nationalism', *Planet* (Tregaron, Wales), June

'Spleáchas: Galar Chonnacht' in *Iarthar na hÉireann agus an Comhphobal Eorpach*, eag. Diarmuid Ó Cearbhaill (Bearna: Oficina Typographica)

1979   'Could Ulster's Advantage Lie in a Federal Ireland Shaped by Ulstermen?', *Church of Ireland Gazette*, 9 February

1981   'The Last Years of the Gaeltacht', *The Crane Bag*, Vol. 5, No. 2 (reprinted in *Heresy*)
        'Can a Shrinking Linguistic Minority Be Saved?' in *Minority Languages Today*, eds E. Haugen, J.D. McClure and D.S. Thompson (Edinburgh University Press)

1982   'History in the Post-Primary School', *Lumen*, Vol. 1, No. 1
        'The Northern Ireland Problem: Basic Data and Terminology', *Études Irlandaises* (Lille), December

1983   'Ireland's Low Morale', *Reality*, February
        'Submission to the New Ireland Forum', in *New Ireland Forum* (Dublin: Government Publications)
        'The Church and Morale', *Reality*, April

1984   'Nuclear Disarmament: A Pro-Life Movement', *Faith* (Esher, Surrey)
        'Northern Ireland: Five Approaches to a Solution' in *How to Save the World – A Fourth World Guide to the Politics of Scale*, eds Nicholas Albery and Yvo Peeters (London: Fourth World Educational Trust)
        'Exploring Zen in Japan', *Martial Arts* (Dublin), Jan-March

1985   'The Humanism of Connolly and AE', *The Crane Bag*, Vol. 9, No 1. (reprinted in *Heresy*)
        'Irish Socialist Thought' in *The Irish Mind*, ed. R. Kearney (Dublin: Wolfhound) (reprinted in *Heresy*)
        'The Relationship of the New Irish Nation to Gaelic since the 19th Century' in *Entstehung von Sprachen und Völkern*, ed. P. Sture Ureland (Tübingen: Niemeyer)

1986   'Creating A New Irish Identity', *Studies*, Winter

1988   'Towards a World Community of Communities' in
          Across the Frontiers, ed. R. Kearney (Dublin:
          Wolfhound) (reprinted in *Heresy*)
          'Joyce's Strange Non-Encounter with the Adriatic',
          Most (Zagreb)
          'Against Revisionism', *The Irish Review*, Spring

1991   'Whatever You Say, Say Nothing: Why Seamus
          Heaney is No. 1', *Stand Magazine* (Newcastle-upon-
          Tyne), Autumn 1981

1992   'Language and Society' in *Essays on Class and Culture in
          Ireland*, eds Séamus Mac Grianna and P.E.S. Ua
          Conchubhair (Derry: University of Ulster)

1994   'A Critic's Response' in *New Works by Knuttel* (Dublin:
          New Apollo Gallery)

1995   'The Shape of Irish Studies in the United States',
          Éire/Ireland (St Paul, Minn.), Spring

1997   'A Fragile World: Postwestern Civilisation', *Studies*,
          Autumn
          'A Provincial Passion: Cleansing Irish Literature of
          Irishness', *Éire/Ireland* (Morristown, NJ),
          Summer/Fall

1998   'Don't Try to Play Golf Where There Are No Golf
          Courses', *Asylum* (Tralee), Vol. 6
          'The Recent Birth and Chequered Career of "Rural
          Ireland"', *InCognito* (Dublin), Vol. 4

'The Challenge of Postwestern Civilisation', *Céide* (Ballina), July / August

'The Postwestern Condition', *Graph* (Dublin), Autumn / Winter

1999   'Three Views of Reality: The Poetry of Higgins, Kavanagh and Heaney', *Incognito* (Dublin), Vol. 5

'Why I will live anywhere but Ireland', *Force 10* (Sligo), Issue 10

'La Fragilità della civiltà postoccidentale', *Transgressioni* (Firenze), No. 28

2000   'The German Influence on Western Culture', *Cultura Tedesca* (Rome), July